U N D E R   D E A D M A N ' S   S K I N

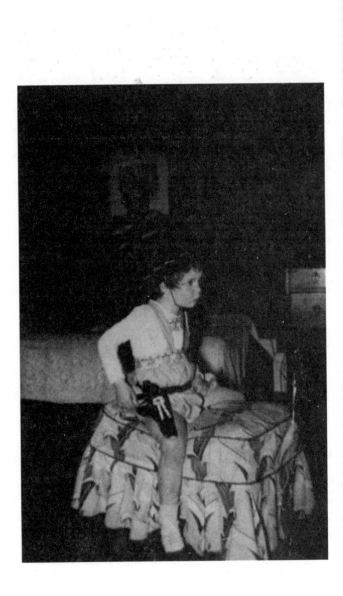

Under Deadman's Skin

Discovering the Meaning of Children's Violent Play

JANE KATCH

Introduction by Vivian Gussin Paley

Beacon Press

BOSTON

Beacon Press
25 Beacon Street
Boston, Massachusetts 02108-2892
www.beacon.org

Beacon Press books
are published under the auspices of
the Unitarian Universalist Association of Congregations.

05 04 03 02 01   8 7 6 5 4 3 2

This book is printed on acid-free paper that meets the uncoated paper
ANSI/NISO specifications for permanence as revised in 1992.

Composition by Wilsted & Taylor Publishing Services

Library of Congress Cataloging-in-Publication Data

Katch, Jane.
    Under deadman's skin : discovering the meaning of children's violent
play / Jane Katch ; introduction by Vivian Gussin Paley.
        p.cm.
"Beacon Press books are published under the auspices of the Unitarian
Universalist Association of Congregations."
Includes bibliographical references and index.
    ISBN 0-8070-3128-3 (hard : alk. paper)
    1. Children and violence. 2. Violence in children. 3. Social
groups. I. Paley, Vivian Gussin. II. Title.
    HQ784.V55 K38 2001
    303.6′083—dc21
                        00-009583

FOR MY MOTHER,
GOLDIE SILVERMAN

AND IN MEMORY OF MY FATHER,
MORRIS SILVERMAN

I TRIED TO OMIT ALL NEEDLESS WORDS
BUT HE WOULD HAVE
CAUGHT THE ONES I MISSED.

CONTENTS

The fantasies of young boys are little tolerated in school these days. The perception of increased real violence in the country has created an inhospitable setting for the pretend stuff. It takes courage for a teacher to allow children to play out the latest scenarios racing around in their heads. More likely the students are warned, "Don't even think about it! No weapons, not even cardboard ones! And no fingers!" The boys are barely able to hold back their explosions until the teachers are out of range.

The fact that Jane Katch chooses not to ban violent images from her kindergarten and first-grade classroom does not reflect a lack of concern. On the contrary, this year the play worries her more than ever. It is filled with "R-rated" material; the boys brag about the mysterious "R" the way their older brothers once proclaimed Good and Evil in hushed tones. Today's play is more visceral and earthy, deliberately "weird" and scary. A game called Suicide is a current favorite in her classroom.

Much as Ms. Katch is tempted to tell the children not to think about it or at least not to *say* it, conscience and curiosity propel her in another direction. After several decades of watching young boys play out their "I'm more powerful and dangerous than you" fantasies, she wonders if the male half of her class has all but eliminated the "hero" and substituted a faceless, tasteless, gory version that the children cannot seem to erase from their collective thoughts.

This being the case, decides Ms. Katch, let the children join her in studying a phenomenon that holds them hostage. Instead of eliminating the script, make it a focus of classroom discourse: How are we to gain control over these worrisome yet tantalizing fantasies?

Jane Katch is eminently qualified for the task. Her training, before she entered a "regular" classroom, took place in the famed Orthogenic School at the University of Chicago, under the careful scrutiny of Bruno Bettelheim. It was from "Dr. B." she learned that to begin dealing with difficult children she must first recall her own childhood terrors and attempt to make connections. Through such self-knowledge would emerge the single most necessary quality in the relationship between adult and child: empathy. It is a word much used in the modern schoolhouse but seldom applied when the going gets rough.

Indeed, how does one empathize with games called Suicide and conversations about cut-up body parts on the way to a math lesson? Does this dark classroom theater portend misshapen psyches to come or, rather, is it the children's ability to make play out of images they should never have been allowed to see—and learn to talk about them—that protects them from despair?

As Ms. Katch struggles to rekindle the ofttimes harsh wisdom of the legendary Dr. B., she rediscovers the childhood disguises she herself invented to ward off the nameless fears of a seemingly safer time. How different in meaning are the camouflages her students now employ, she asks herself, as she helps them create a community in which their feelings and their play can be openly discussed within the context of an ongoing school curriculum.

The subject of the continuing dialogue appears to be "what shall be done about this play of ours that excites us but also causes so much tension?" The evidence and possibilities are straightforwardly put before us in the children's own words.

To the universal debate over the effects of media violence on the young, Jane Katch's voice is a model of well-reasoned self-examination and of faith in the capacity of children to do the same. She is a teacher of uncommon sensitivity, honesty, and skill.

Under Deadman's Skin is a remarkable book about the role of fantasy play in our troubled times, but, reading between the lines, we see that it is really about the art of teaching and learning in a democratic classroom.

Vivian Gussin Paley

CHAPTER I

The Suicide Game

The five- and six-year-olds in my class have invented a new game called Suicide. They play it in the room when they've finished their work, and outdoors at recess. I have never seen a game I hate so much in which all the children involved are so happy. It follows our three classroom rules for violence in play, rules the children and I have made and refined together, and to which they carefully adhere: no excessive blood, no cutting off of body parts, and no guts spilled. It also follows our rule about what the children have labeled "mushy stuff": the people in their stories cannot take off their clothes. Animals can. But the suicide game does get very noisy, so when I look for an excuse to stop it, that is the only one I can find.

"This game is too loud!" I tell the four players one morning. "I'm trying to have a reading group, and we can't hear each other. You'll have to stop, clean up the mess, and make a different choice. You can play this game later, outside."

"But we like this!" Seth argues. One of the tallest children in the class, he stands straight and looks me in the eye. His recent short haircut accentuates his new older-boy look.

"Can we stay in the drama area but play a different game?" Seth's best friend, Daniel, asks.

"You can try that, but if it's still too loud, you'll have to choose one of the table activities, like art or small blocks," I relent a bit.

"Let's play Suicide," I hear Seth say as I walk away.

"That's what we were playing," Gregory answers.

Where did they learn about suicide, these six-year-olds? I look around the room. At the art table, children make clothes and beds for their Beanie Babies. In the block area, the kittens are building traps for the mice. Why does a group of apparently normal, happy children choose to play Suicide?

"Let's make Bernie come to outer space," Seth suggests. Bernie is Gregory's imaginary friend and the main character in most of his stories. I wonder if Gregory will object to this treatment.

"Yeah!" Daniel says enthusiastically. "Me and Seth are space aliens!"

"Bernie commits suicide." Gregory gives his approval.

"There's two Bernies and two aliens," Daniel says, clarifying the structure of the game.

Nina joins the plans. "I'll be a Bernie, I guess." She sounds a bit reluctant, but she is Gregory's best friend and wants to be his ally.

"I can take on Gregory," Seth says to Daniel. "You take on Nina."

I know they haven't really changed the game as they promised. They've just moved into outer space, further away from critical teachers. But they are, for the moment, quiet, and the children in my reading group are doing well on their own, so I continue to eavesdrop, hoping no parents enter the room. I don't think they'd approve of the suicide game.

"We have special seats that you guys go in, and we make you commit suicide," Daniel explains.

"Now, sit on that chair," Seth commands to Gregory. "We can blow you up! S-s-s-s-s-s-s! Now! Commit suicide!"

"You have to be funny, like, so silly." Daniel adds a new dimension.

Gregory understands immediately, and starts talking baby talk.

"Okay, Bernie." Seth takes over. "Here's an apple."

"An apple!" gurgles Gregory happily, taking the plastic food. "Goo, goo!" he adds, taking a pretend bite. They all laugh loudly.

"It's really a hand grenade. Do you know you're gonna explode, Gregory? It's gonna kill you!" Their laughter contrasts sharply with their words, making the scene even more macabre and disturbing to me, but Gregory appears unconcerned. "I'm gonna commit suicide to myself," he chortles. "Eeee!" He explodes happily onto the floor.

"That was fun," Seth reports. "We're the masters. If you killed your master, you would die anyway," he tells Gregory, who is getting up for another round. "Want a ball?"

Will Gregory, a highly competitive boy who always must be on the winning team, continue to accept the slave role?

"Yeah!" he says enthusiastically.

Seth hands Gregory a plastic plate. "I didn't say, 'Ball.' I said, 'Bomb!'" They all laugh. He looks at me. "Can we put on a play of this, for the whole class?"

"No," I say without explanation.

"Aw," Seth complains. He scribbles on a piece of paper and turns back to Gregory. "Now this note says if you don't commit suicide, you'll be dead for a whole year!" He folds the paper and hands it over. "Follow me or I'll shoot you!"

Why do Gregory and Nina, usually such imaginative, constructive leaders in the class, want to be helpless victims in the grip of this alien sadistic force? Is the thrill of Seth's latest violent fantasy too exciting to resist? I must stop this game. I can, at least, banish it to the playground, where I don't have to hear it or give it my seal of approval by allowing it.

At our next class meeting, I announce an abrupt change of rules to the children. "When you play games that are violent," I tell them, "it's too hard for you to settle down. Since math always begins right after recess, on some days it is hard for you to concentrate on your work."

"That's just because we haven't finished our game," Seth explains.

"I understand. But from now on, when you play pretend indoors, I want you to play games that are not violent and have no shooting or killing in them."

"Can't we have no blood, just shooting?" Seth asks, reminding me of our class agreement.

"No."

"Can't you go, 'Ch-ch-ch'? Quietly?" asks Nina.

"No."

Seth shoots at Daniel across the rug. "Ch-ch-ch."

"I'm going to close the drama area if you do that," I say firmly. The space for dramatic play, including dress-ups and the house area, is one of the most popular choices in the room, and the children sit up straighter, realizing how serious I am. They all start talking at once, surprised at my abrupt change of rules.

"Can we play a game with wild animals in the jungle?" Nina asks.

"If it's not too wild," I answer.

"Can we hunt with bows and arrows?"

"We can try hunting," I relent.

"How 'bout animals tear up people?" Daniel asks.

"No," I say firmly.

"We'll cut them up," Seth whispers to him.

"No," I say. "You won't."

The discussion over, I am relieved. For once, I will act the way other teachers do and just prohibit the awful stuff.

After school, I complain to the principal, telling her about the new game and my authoritarian response to it. She listens thoughtfully. "You must have worked with violent children when you worked at Bruno Bettelheim's school," she says. "What would he have said about this?"

I am taken by surprise. She is right, of course. Working with emotionally disturbed children for eight years, I must have learned something that could be useful to me now. Yet I've separated that experience into a special compartment, not to be opened.

"I don't know what you learned from him," she goes on, "but whatever it is, it makes your work different."

"How?" I ask, startled.

"It has to do with empathy," she says.

It seems so clear, once she's said it, like something I've always known but didn't want to remember. Why didn't I think about this before, while I was wondering about the violent fantasies of these children?

I know the answer as soon as I hear the question. If I look at those memories, I'll have to see the pain that was there as well as the knowledge I gained. Bettelheim demanded that we learn to understand the children by first looking at our own feelings.

CHAPTER 2

Murderer

"So, you vanted to murder Brenda!" Dr. B., as we all called him, stared at me with his big dark eyes that seemed to pop out from his large head. It was my first day working alone, and my first Wednesday night staff meeting. I had been instructed to get the eight children in my group to bed early, so I could be sure to be in the staff room by 8:45. I was on time, but it had been difficult. The adolescent girls had behaved very differently than they had when I had spent the week observing them with an experienced counselor. With me, the new substitute, they had been critical and angry, disapproving of almost everything about me. I was just out of college, only a few years older than they were. I was looking forward to putting the lights out early, but when Brenda kept putting off getting to bed, I ran out of time and patience and just turned out the light, did my last cleanup chores, and went to the meeting, relieved to be through for the day.

"You vould like to do away vith her?" Dr. B. repeated.

Frantically, I went over the day in my mind, looking for anything that could make him think I was a child murderer. Could one of the children have complained to Dr. B. about the abrupt lights-out when he made his nightly rounds of the dorms? Would that make him think I wanted to murder her?

What was I supposed to do when Brenda wouldn't get into bed? Did I really want to do away with her? Could he be right? Maybe I did wish she didn't exist, as she silently ignored my requests to get ready for bed, putting me in the position of neglecting her or being late for the most important meeting of the week.

"I don't know," I mumbled, confused.

"You must find out, eh?" he demanded. "If you vant to understand the murderous fantasies of these difficult children, first you must be villing to look at your own!"

An unusual way to learn empathy.

Can I make a place in school for understanding these fantasies, instead of shutting them out? Could the children and I study violence together? Could we see when their play helps them learn and when it interferes with their schoolwork?

CHAPTER 3

Rated R

I'm washing yesterday's brushes, putting them in baby food jars full of paint on the art table and savoring my last moments of morning solitude as the children start coming into my classroom in twos and threes.

"Anybody knows he's dead, right?" The intensity of Seth's voice breaks through my thoughts. "He goes over a lumpy force field. I've seen part two of it. Part two is awesome. A dead man says, 'Give me that money.' The guy says, 'All right, butthead.' And the other one says, 'Who are you calling that?' And he says, 'Ooh! Ooooh!' And then he sticks out his hand and grabs his heart and rips it out."

I turn around to look at Seth. Watching the top of his blond head bent over a stack of empty cereal boxes, I am reminded that this intense adolescent male voice comes, in fact, from a six-year-old body, just losing its roundness and becoming tall and lanky. Daniel works next to him, pushing his black straight hair out of his dark eyes, to get a better view of the best position for the Popsicle sticks he is attaching with the glue gun so they will point out in all directions from the cereal boxes. In Seth's pause, Daniel answers softly, "Yeah, but ghosts don't have hearts."

Seth doesn't miss a beat as he continues his narrative. "Yeah, but Deadman did that to another guy. Know what's under Deadman's skin? Know what's under his skin? It's bones and blood. He's got people's everything. Daniel, have you seen the movie, *Deadman*?"

"No," Daniel admits.

"Good," Seth continues. "It's gory! And it's rated R, right? You can't even see rated R*s,* can you? Can you see rated R*s,* Kayla? You don't want to see rated R. You don't want to see *Deadman.* It's totally gore-y, right?" Kayla has come in quietly and is cutting fabric for a dress for a clothespin doll. "I know why it's rated R," she says, flipping her blond braids behind her shoulders. "He ripped off a hand. Who cares?" she adds casually. Kayla has two big brothers and she knows how to talk to boys.

"No, he didn't!" Seth tells her. "You never seen *Deadman.*"

Kayla holds her ground. "Yeah, but I heard you guys talking about it."

"Yeah," Seth answers, "but that was a part I made up, right, Daniel? Yeah, you haven't seen *Deadman,* so you don't know. I've seen *Deadman* at my friend's house," he goes on. "All it is, is a murderer says, 'I'll kill you, I'll kill you, I'll kill you!' You don't want to see *Deadman.* It's just talking."

"Yeah," Daniel agrees. "It only has a few violents in it. Like two or three."

Like Kayla, I find it hard to know where the movie script ends and Seth's embellishments begin. I've never been able to watch violent movies. I don't even like to watch the news. I prefer to listen to it on the radio and avoid the visual images that I find so disturbing when I lie down to go to sleep.

"There's six swears in it," Seth continues. "There's twelve swears in it."

"I don't care." Kayla tells him.

"Just don't see it," he says. "It's boring."

Six swears or twelve, I don't want to hear about them at the art table. Kayla's mother took me aside last week to complain about the language Kayla's been bringing home. "I'm sending Kayla here, to a private school," she told me sternly, "because I didn't want her with the rough kids in the neighborhood. But from what she's telling me, I'm not sure. . . . "

"They are nice children," I assured her. "They work and play well together. But I will talk with them about their language."

In my irritation, both at Seth and at Kayla's mother, I forget my new resolve to listen and to try to understand. "Remember," I tell Seth, "we agreed not to talk about violent stuff at school."

"It's totally boring." Seth may be agreeing with me, but I'm not sure.

"Oh, Daniel," he goes on. "Have you seen Bloodman? Bloodman is all red. He has red eyes, and know what he can do? Say, he could turn into blood and you could go in it. You could get really, really sick."

"Seth," I say more firmly this time. "We're not doing that anymore. It upsets other children in the class, and it doesn't follow our rule about blood!"

It also upsets me. Where does he get this information? Has he seen the movies or the previews? Does he hear it from older boys? Or is he making it all up?

I remember when I was the age of these rated-R watchers. We had just got our first television set, and the only kids' shows were *Howdy Doody* and *Kukla, Fran and Ollie.* Violence was when the Lone Ranger shot the bad guy. There was no blood on black and white TV. One of my early photographs shows me wearing my fringed leather cowgirl skirt and vest, my cap gun cocked and pointed, peeking out carefully at the television from behind a big wing chair. I liked the safety of knowing I could make a quick escape if I needed to.

"Joel," Seth says to a boy who is gluing Popsicle sticks on the other side of the art table. "Don't you think Bloodman is even scarier than *I Still Know What You Did Last Summer*? Right? This scene is scare-y! Joel, can you see rated-R movies?"

"Yeah," Joel answers, pushing his glasses back on his nose as he bends over his work.

"Oh yeah?" Seth's voice has a rough, confrontational tone now. "What'd you see that's rated R?"

"I saw *Men in Black*," Joel says.

He is a year younger and several inches shorter than Seth, but he answers confidently.

"That's not rated R," Seth announces. "It's PG-13. It was just a little violence, right, Daniel? You gonna see part two? I almost died. My mom almost had a heart attack when she saw it. She almost fainted." He pauses a moment. "She fainted when she saw it. Duh! And then I watched the whole thing by myself!"

I do not take any of Seth's accounts literally. Advertisements, previews, or conversations of the older boys on the bus may form the outlines of the images that are filled in by his imagination. Yet I feel haunted by this fainthearted mother who is unable to protect him from his own wish to see the movies that preoccupy and fascinate him.

Uninvited, an image appears in my mind, from a show I saw when I was the age of Seth and Daniel. A girl was playing hopscotch on the sidewalk in front of her house. As she bent over to write with the chalk, the camera zoomed closer and I saw she was writing down the number of children kidnapped by a murderer still on the loose. As she wrote, a man's shadow loomed above her, bent closer, and I knew she would be his next victim.

I had assumed that the program was the news. Only today, viewing the image through my adult eyes, do I realize my mistake.

As I watch Seth now, mixing fantasy and reality in every sentence, I see him as the young six-year-old he is, not the adolescent I heard a little while before. Is he trying to cover his fear of the unknown with this incessant boasting? I imagine him watching these violent movies at home, not knowing what is real and what is pretend, and wish I could give him a big old wing chair to hide behind.

CHAPTER 4

The Party

"Seth," I tell him sternly as he continues his work at the art table. "I don't want you showing off about the scary movies you've seen. If you do, I'll have you find a different activity and I'll separate you from your friends."

I will not behave like his imaginary helpless mother, fainting during a violent movie, unable to set limits or to protect him.

My school day begins with a time for the children to choose their own activities. It's my favorite part of the day. I love to watch their intense involvement with their projects and see the growth of their ability to work together. Until this year, I've never had to censor language. I've always found that bad language disappears most quickly if I make little of it. I just explain that it's not appropriate in the classroom, ignore the occasional bathroom talk if it's not in my direct earshot, and it goes away. But this year, something is different. The sex and violence in the children's talk is increasing. I've even wondered if I should begin the day with a structured work time.

"This is a cannonball shooter," Joel's clear young voice brings me back to the present as he tries to show Seth the elaborate Popsicle stick structure he has made. Seth seems to ignore Joel, just as he ignored my first requests for a change in subject.

"Daniel," he whispers urgently. "This turns into a battleship. We can tell them it turns into a battleship. We just can't tell them *how* it turns into a battleship."

Following Seth's instructions, Daniel turns to Joel. "This turns into a battleship," he announces.

Joel is pleased to be included. "Remember," he answers, "I'm still on your team."

But I am not sure that they do remember. Seth prefers to play with only one child at a time, and most days the chosen one is not Joel.

"It's not that way," Seth tells him, emphasizing each word. "It's at my *house,* right? It's a *party,* right, Daniel—"

"That's not fair!" Kayla interrupts. "If you're talking about it in school, you have to invite everyone!"

"That's right," I back her up quickly. "Remember our agreement: if everyone's not invited, you can't talk about it." I know this party may not actually exist, but the rule is still important to both Kayla and me.

"We're inviting everybody to the *party,* right?" Seth checks with Daniel. "I just don't know how many can *sleep over.*"

"Yeah," Daniel agrees.

I seem to have been effective, for the moment, in stopping the talk of violence. But is this new subject an improvement? Seth's need for power seems to have switched from mastering the details of Deadman, to forging an alliance with Daniel that keeps Joel excluded.

"Daniel," Seth continues, "at my party, it's gonna be cool! We can have candy! We're gonna have movies and movies, stay up late, watch Nickelodeon."

"Can you stay up late?" Daniel asks, impressed. He is a full year younger than Seth, and is pleased to be included by the older boy. "I'm gonna sleep over? Want me to bring my biggest sleeping bag?"

"We're gonna sleep outside," Seth explains.

"In a tent?" Daniel asks.

"Yeah," Seth elaborates. "We'll surf the Net."

"I don't know if I can sleep over," Daniel answers. Sleeping outside has him worried. And who knows what surfing the Net might mean to a five-year-old imagination.

"Bring your video games," Seth directs him, ignoring the fact that Daniel might not be coming. "Bring your Nintendo."

"I'll bring my Little Mermaid game," Daniel says. "It's hard to beat."

Seth leans toward Kayla. "I can't wait to tease Daniel 'cause he has a Little Mermaid game," he tells her in a stage whisper.

Kayla turns to me. "He's teasing," she announces on cue.

"When you come over to my house for a party," Seth continues, ignoring her, "it's gonna be the best, radical, awesome party. And at the end, Daniel, know what we're gonna do, when everybody else is gone, you're gonna stay *all night*. Plus, Daniel, let's get brainwashed! We'll eat popcorn, Oreos. . . . And I'll bring my spear!"

I am about to imagine what he meant by "let's get brainwashed," but the spear demands my full attention.

"You have a real spear?" Daniel asks, awed.

"No, a fake one," Seth admits. He pauses only briefly. "But it's sharper than a needle."

I know that Seth's mother allows no weapons in the house, real or pretend. She's told me that she and her husband do not understand where Seth's fascination with violence comes from. Their attempts to limit the violence in his fantasy play have been as unsuccessful as my attempts to stop his violent language. Could Seth have picked up such violent talk just from television advertisements and from the older boys he admires on the school bus? Or were his parents being less than honest with me or with themselves?

"Who wants my cannonball shooter?" Joel holds up his finished Popsicle stick product.

"Me!"

"Me!"

Both Seth and Daniel admire his work across the table.

"You can both have it," Joel tells them diplomatically.

"I'm taking it home," Seth says. "What are those guns for?" he asks Joel, looking at another of Joel's constructions. "For my cannonball shooter?"

"No, I'm making a light saber," Joel explains, holding it up. The long, intricate design of the Popsicle sticks is a work of art, even to my eyes.

"For me?" Seth asks, excitedly.

"No, it's for Nina's Star Wars show."

"No!" Seth demands. "Can you make one for me? Is this one for me?"

But Joel stands firm. "No, it's for the show."

"How 'bout this, Joel? I get to take it home, except Nina uses it for the show."

"No," Joel answers. As much as he wants to be on their team, he is unwilling to compromise his promise to Nina, who is a leader in her sphere as Seth is in his. And Seth's clear admiration for Joel's work continues, even through Joel's rejection of his demand. I admire the way Joel has changed the balance of power and yet remained true to his sense of what he wanted for himself. In contrast, my interventions accomplish at best only a short-term change in the subject of the boys' discussions. I know the talk of violence will continue as soon as they go to recess, or when they think I am out of earshot. As much as I want to continue cutting off their talk as soon as it becomes violent, if I'm going to make any real changes I'm going to have to understand their play. And that means that first, I have to listen.

CHAPTER 5

Runaways

The children are outdoors at recess and I am using the half hour of quiet time to set up a math activity and drink an uninterrupted cup of coffee, when Joel runs into the room, breathless with excitement.

"Seth, Nina, and Daniel ran away," he announces.

"What do you mean?" I ask, pausing in my work, puzzled but not alarmed.

"They said they were running away and they went out the front door," he explains.

"I'm sure it's a game," I reassure him. To myself, I think that Nina would never do something that would get her in that much trouble. She is too levelheaded. "They must be just pretending to run away," I tell Joel.

"No." He insists. "They're really doing it."

Just to be sure, I check the bathrooms, to see if they're playing hide-and-seek. I tell Joel I'll come out to recess as soon as I'm done setting up for math. I'm confident that by then they'll have turned up in some nook and cranny of the playground.

Seth tests the rules. He might run away to see what would happen, or to be able to boast about it to his friends. Daniel would follow him anywhere. But Nina is a leader of good play in the class and a fine student as well. She knows the rules, and wants everyone to follow them so that work and play will go smoothly.

Out at recess a few minutes later, I find the teachers are concerned. No one has been able to find Seth, Nina, or Daniel. Just as I walk toward the office to report them missing, the gym teacher walks in with them, holding Seth and Nina firmly by the hand, with Daniel a step behind. "I found them walking down the road toward town," he tells me, "when I was driving back from the store. They told me they could walk back to school alone, but I disagreed." He hides a fleeting smile.

I sit them down on chairs outside the principal's office. "What were you doing?" I ask.

There is a long pause. I stare unrelentingly at Nina, knowing that Seth is unlikely to speak first.

"We were going to camp out," Nina finally says quietly, staring at the lunch box on her lap. "We thought we could sleep in empty cars." Her boyish straight brown hair almost hides her face, making it hard to hear what she is saying.

"Why did you do it?" I look at Seth this time.

"I must have been out of my mind" is all he tells me.

"Yeah, me too," Daniel echoes.

I go into the principal's office to tell her what has happened.

"I don't understand it," I say. "Seth's always testing the rules, but why would Nina use such bad judgment?"

I imagine the effect the news will have on my class. "Seth and Nina are leaders in the class, and if they come back and brag about their adventures, the idea will catch on like wildfire," I tell her. "Do you think you should call their parents, have them come in and talk with you, and then take the children home for the day?" She agrees to the plan, and I go back to class to tell the children what happened.

"I heard Nina talking about running away," Gregory explains, "but I thought it was just pretend." He nervously chews on his fingernails.

"If you do think someone is not following a rule, and you think it might be dangerous," I explain to the children, "it's important to tell an adult."

"My brother always calls me a tattletale," Kayla says, "when I tell my mother on him."

"My mom says if someone could get hurt, you need to tell," Alison says. "One day, my friend wanted to go down the hill where you're never supposed to go. I went up the hill as fast as I could to tell her mom. My friend was just a little mad."

"Seth, Daniel, and Nina might have been hurt, walking to town by themselves," I explain. "If you help keep your friends safe, you're being a good friend, not a tattletale."

"I told you they were running away," Joel points out. "Even though they told me not to."

The principal comes in to tell us that Seth, Nina, and Daniel have been taken home for the day. She tells us that the parents have decided that Nina's birthday party next week, to which they have all been invited, has been canceled, and that the other two children will not have parties this year, either.

The children are shocked. They didn't know anyone could lose a birthday party.

All day I puzzle about Nina. Most comfortable with boys, she enjoys active play. She keeps the games she's in on a tight rope: they're fun but never out of control. Once I watched her pretending to be the mother in a game of house. Her two fussy babies were crawling on the floor, fighting over the play telephone. "No one will use the phone," she told them sternly, picking it up and putting it on top of the play refrigerator.

Nina's not the kind of girl who runs up to hug me in the morning, but I believe we have a mutual respect for each other. She handles most problems herself, but I count on her to tell me if there's something going on that I should know.

I am still thinking about her the next morning before school, when Nate walks into my room. Nate was in my class four years ago, and he likes to stop in to check things out on the days he comes to school early to get extra help with his reading.

"I heard about your kids running away yesterday," he comments as he watches me cut colored paper into quarter sheets. "I think it has to do with the movies they watch," he adds.

"What do you mean?" I ask, startled, looking up at him. "Were they talking about movies?"

"No," he tells me. "But I remember when I was their age, I saw *Home Alone 2* and I watched Kevin slide down the banister. Well, one night, we were on vacation and the hotel had a long banister and this marble floor at the bottom. It looked like the movie. Dad was playing a game with me, I think. He went, 'Rrrrr,' as he came up the stairs. Or maybe it was just the loud noise of his feet. But I decided I was like Kevin and he was the robber. I thought I could slide down the banister just like Kevin did in the movie. Except he didn't fall off, and I did." He pauses. "I know it was dangerous, but right then, I was Kevin, and I didn't think about it."

Was he "out of his mind," too, I wonder, remembering Seth's description of his running away.

"What happened?" I ask Nate. "I don't remember you being hurt when you were in my class."

"No. Luckily my mom was at the bottom of the stairs and she caught me! There's all kinds of movies," he explains to me. "Kids running away from parents, kids doing wicked things. I think maybe the little kids shouldn't watch them."

I think I agree. I was convinced that a movie kidnapper was real, and Nate believed he was Kevin. Seth and Nina could have been playing out a script from a movie and forgotten it was just pretend.

CHAPTER 6

Obsessed

Since Nina, Seth, and Daniel seem unable to explain why they ran away, I decide to talk with some other older children; those, like Nate, who are young enough to remember how they felt at five, but old enough to be able to articulate their thoughts and ideas more clearly. I ask Nate's teacher if I might come into her class to talk with the children about violence and play. She, too, is concerned about the fascination some of her children have with violence, and she is quick to arrange a time.

I go to her room with two questions in mind. First, do the children, like Nate, think watching violent movies encourages young children to lose their good judgment? And second, does movie watching encourage a fascination with violence that makes it hard for some young children to get the images out of their minds?

I walk into the group of nine- and ten-year-olds a bit nervously, not knowing how I will be received. As I look at their eager faces, I realize that many of them were in my class when they were five or six, and I immediately feel more comfortable in this alien environment.

I explain to them that when I was little, my brother and I played Davy Crockett, King of the Wild Frontier, or Captain Hook and Peter Pan. We fought the pirates or the Indians, using our fingers for guns, or a cap gun, if we were lucky enough to have one. There was not much violent talk in our games, other than

"Bang, bang, you're dead" or "Walk the plank!" There was not much explicit violence on television, either, since dead Indians, cowboys, or pirates usually fell bloodless to the ground.

"I'm interested in how play is changing," I tell the children.

"I love violent movies," a boy named Jason answers, eager to talk. "If you see a movie you really like, you play stuff based on that movie. If you see a James Bond movie with all the shooting, you play games with more shooting. I used to be obsessed with that. I couldn't stop it."

I find myself immediately fascinated by Jason's professed obsession. His intensity mirrors Seth's, although Jason's voice lacks Seth's defiant tone.

Ross, more hesitant in his manner, speaks next. "I don't know if I like violent movies," he says slowly, " 'cause I've practically never seen one. And my little brother can't. But he'll watch *Power Rangers* or something like that, and he'll actually act like it! He goes, 'I'm gonna shoot you!' He tries to wrestle me."

"Do you think he does it because of the movie?" I ask him.

"He probably wouldn't have done it if he didn't watch the movie," Ross tells me. "For some people, like my brother, it makes them act violent."

I have so many questions. Who are these "people" who may have this tendency? Do the movies today, with their more explicit violence, encourage children to act violent? Is it only "some people" who are affected this way? And what can parents do to prevent this?

"Some parents let their kids watch whatever they want," I say. "And other parents don't let their kids see anything violent. What's the effect of telling kids, 'You can't watch anything violent on television'? Does it make them less violent? Or does it make them want to watch it more?"

"I've never seen a PG-13 movie at all," Ross explains. "My parents don't let me and I don't want to. I play games from what other people say about the movies." I knew Ross when he was five, and even then, he was content to follow another child's script.

"I don't think movies make you violent," Nate says. "That has to do with what you're brought up to when you're seven or eight. Movies like that just give you nightmares. They scare me to heck."

"When I'm watching a movie," a boy named Brandon speaks for the first time, "and there's a scary part coming and my mom says, 'You shouldn't watch this,' or she says, 'Close your eyes,' because it's too violent, you want to see it. Or it's a preview, and you can't wait to see it, 'cause your parents won't let you."

"When your parents make you close your eyes, that's when you *want to see it*?" Ross asks, puzzled. His television would already be turned off at that point, I am sure, so this would not happen at his house.

"That's when you *do* open your eyes," Brandon explains. "You just keep them wide open."

I wonder if the consistent prohibition in Ross's family makes it easier for him to be uninterested in violence, or whether his lack of interest makes it easier for his parents to enforce the prohibition.

"The kids in my class are five and six," I tell them. "What are your recommendations for them?"

"It's kinda like up to the parents," Brandon begins. "Like eventually, they're gonna learn about people getting shot and guts and things like that. But it's just bad to see a movie like that early, 'cause it could give them nightmares."

"There's one movie, *Titanic*," says Claire, the first girl to speak. "A lot of people have seen that, and they're talking about it a lot, and I still don't want to see it 'cause there's people drowning. I don't like to see violence."

"In *Amistad*," Jason says, "it's like real violent, and there's really a lot of gore. I thought about it after I saw it. It's different from a movie that has a lot of violence and swears just for effect. In *Amistad*, the violence shows how it really was; they're trying to tell you something."

I want to hear more about Jason and Brandon's passion for violence. They sound the way I imagine Seth might in a few years, still interested in violence but able to articulate his feelings more clearly. "If there are kids who are five or six or seven," I ask, "who have a consuming interest in violence, what can adults do?"

"My obsession happened for about two months," Jason explains. "When I had it, I thought everything that didn't have to do with blasting someone's guts out was boring. Now, a lot of the stuff I think about has to do with killing. Last year I was interested in vampires, but I had other interests, too. What you really have to do," he continues, "is just let them wait. They'll outgrow it. But you also say, 'I don't like the way you're doing this.' You explain to them what violence is and why it's not good. That's what my dad did. He got upset when he saw all the violence in my games and in the stories I was writing and he talked to me about it."

I look at the clock and at the hands raised in front of me of the children who have more to say. "I should leave now," I tell them. They look surprised and disappointed. I feel that way too, as though I'm just beginning to break through their ideas of what they think I want to hear, and to get more honest reactions from the children. "Your teacher and I had agreed I would stay for a half hour. Maybe I could come back another day, if I can't go on now?" I ask.

"Go on! Go on!" the children say. I look at the teacher. She nods.

"What the parents should do," Ross tells me, "is just say no, no, no, no, no, so they'll just give up. That's what they do to me, and I'm not violent."

"Once you see a few violent movies," Brandon says, "sort of like, you get addicted to it. Then you start playing violent games, and you get toy guns. You pretend you're like James Bond, and you have little ropes and you tie them to trees and try to swing off them. I don't think it's good. When you're old enough, like ten, you know not to do stuff like that. And you know when they jump off trains, someone's really throwing a dummy off a train. But when you're little, you sort of get addicted and you start doing that stuff and you go to school and you punch a kid. When I was little, there was a shed about as high as the ceiling and I said, 'The guys on shows do this when they jump off trains,' so I jumped off the shed. . . . I could barely walk the next morning."

The parallel with Nate's *Home Alone* story is striking. Did I ever get so wrapped up in my fantasy play that I forgot it was just pretend? I quickly scan through my memories of my favorite games: Peter Pan, Pocahontas, Robin Hood. "But I'm really just Jane, right?" I asked my mother in the beginning of each game. I kept one foot in the door of reality so I would know who I really was, and not become lost in fantasy.

Sabrina brings me back to the present discussion. "My little sister, she was over at her best friend's house, and I came over to pick her up and she was watching this movie called *Body Snatchers,* and I got her out of there as fast as I could and I told my mother and she's not allowed to watch TV at her friend's house anymore."

"I think that violence comes from being angry," Carly says, looking at the problem from a new angle. "Like if your mom says you're grounded for a week, you could have some violent fantasies."

Jason is interested in the idea. "In my old school, there was a kid and it started out that someone didn't really like him. And then that person who didn't like him started spreading rumors about him and people believed the rumors and made fun of him, and then that kid became mean. And then people didn't like him 'cause he was mean. I think it can sort of make someone violent."

I wonder if Jason is talking about someone else, or if he's describing the beginnings of his own obsession. I want to know more about him, but I hear my own class coming in from recess, and this time I must go.

I have plenty to think about. Several of these children who are nine and ten believe that they would not be harmed by movies that they are certain could be dangerous or disturbing to a child who is five or six. At their age, they imply, they know the difference between fantasy and reality, while the younger children are easily confused. Like Nate playing *Home Alone,* they have memories of becoming so caught up in their fantasies, they temporarily forgot it was just pretend.

Yet even though most of these older children believe that they no longer would make such errors in judgment, and therefore can watch what they like, they value consistency in their parents' rules. Ross agrees with his parents' strict limits, and Brandon criticizes his parents' inconsistencies. These children enjoy seeing themselves as the "big kids" who can handle watching what the young ones should not see. But they also feel protective of the younger ones, and are concerned about them.

I usually try to avoid telling parents how to bring up their children. I see my area of expertise as the classroom: I know how young children learn in school, and how they relate to their peers. Yet this time I am so concerned, I decide to follow the older children's advice and write a letter to the parents of all the children in my class, to ask them to be aware of what their children are watching and to limit their viewing of violent movies as consistently as they can.

> Dear Parents,
>
> I am concerned, as I know many of you are, about the explicit violence in the conversation and play of some of the children in our class. While some children seem fascinated and preoccupied by the violence in movies or television programs they have seen or heard about, others are puzzled or disturbed by the descriptions they have heard from their classmates. This preoccupation seems to be interfering with their ability to concentrate and settle down in school.
>
> In order to understand more about the cause and effect of this fascination with violence, I did some reading about the effects of television on young children. I found that according to a report of the American Psychological Association, many studies have reported a strong link between young children's viewing of violence on television and their aggression. For example, in a classic study by [Albert] Bandura, children who watched more aggressive television programs played more aggressively immediately afterwards than did children who had watched a program that was nonviolent.
>
> The long-term nature of the relationship between television and aggression is less clear. It is difficult to determine whether watching violent programs causes more aggressive behavior later in life or whether children who are more inclined toward violence choose to watch more violent programs when they are young. However, one interesting study, The Impact of Television, found a consistent increase in violent behavior in communities after television was introduced where it had not previously existed.

Who's Calling the Shots, by Nancy Carlsson-Paige, describes the problems related to children's viewing of violent programs, and she gives helpful specific suggestions for parents who would like to set limits and introduce alternatives for their children. I recommend it to you.

After looking at the literature, I talked with a group of older children, to hear what they thought about this issue. Some remembered that when they were five and six, they copied dangerous behavior they saw in movies, forgetting, while they were engrossed in their play, that it was just pretend. These older children believe that parents of younger children should set clear limits on the movies and television their children watch. As one boy told me, "Just say no, no, no, no, no."

Children have been pretending to shoot each other for as long as I can remember. However, there has been a change from "Bang, bang, you're dead!" to playing a game the children call 'Suicide,' and talking about grabbing someone's heart and pulling it out.

I have been hesitant to expand my role as classroom teacher, going beyond a description of how your child learns in the classroom, and moving into making a recommendation to you that affects your child rearing practice. However, from the observations I have made in class, the connections between aggression and television viewing in the literature, and the opinions of the older children I interviewed, it is clear to me that some strong cautions make sense.

I urge you to pay careful attention to what your child sees in the media, and to limit it appropriately. If it is helpful to you, feel free to explain that I am requesting these limits. The children may find it easier to accept the change if they know that "everyone is doing it."

I am including the references for the book and articles I have mentioned, so you can look at them yourself if you are interested.

If you have any concerns or questions about this issue, please do not hesitate to call me. I appreciate your support.

American Psychological Association. *Violence and Youth: Psychology's Response: Vol. 1, Summary Report of the American Psychological Association Commission on Violence and Youth.* Washington, D.C.: American Psychological Association, 1993.

Bandura, A., D. Ross, and S. Ross. "Imitation of Film-Mediated Aggressive Models." *Journal of Abnormal and Social Psychology.* 66 1963: 3–11.

Carlsson-Paige, Nancy. *Who Calling the Shots?: How to Respond Effectively to Children's Fascination with War Play and War Toys*. Philadelphia: New Society Publishers, 1990.

Williams, Tanis M., ed. *The Impact of Television*. Orlando, Fl.: Academic Press, 1986.

The response to the letter surprises me. I get more positive phone calls and comments from the mothers of the children than I have had from any letter I have ever sent home. According to these mothers, they do not allow their own children to watch such violent movies, but they know that other parents in the class do, and they welcome my prohibition. A few mothers tell me that the child's father or another adult took the child to see such a movie without the mother's approval. Others confess that the child has access to cable television in a den or in the child's own room, and the mother does not always know what the child is watching.

I know my letter will not change all these problems, but I hope it will make it easier for the parents to say no, no, no, no, no.

CHAPTER 7

Reserved

"So. Tell me about yourself." Bruno Bettelheim stared at me across his big wooden desk during my first visit to the Orthogenic School in Chicago. I tried to avoid his eyes, and looked instead at the art objects around his office, settling finally on the complete works of Freud behind his left shoulder. I had nothing to say. It wasn't that I was undecided on which of several ways to begin; my mind was simply blank. Didn't I know who I was? I said nothing.

"You are very reserved, you know."

At this understatement, I burst into tears. He let me cry quietly for a while, then walked around his desk and patted me on the shoulder. When I walked out of his office a little later, I was sure I had lost the opportunity to be a counselor at the Orthogenic School. Well, I was just there on a lark. I had sent in my application during Christmas break of my senior year of college, but by May, I expected I would choose instead to make pottery on a craft commune in the Berkshires. When Bettelheim wrote to me offering to pay my airfare to Chicago to visit the school, I figured I had nothing to lose. And even after this disastrous beginning, I decided I might as well finish out the weekend at the school as I had planned.

The next day, I visited with an experienced counselor and a group of adolescent girls. They were rehearsing a scene from a play about Joan of Arc. The girl playing Joan began to cry, telling her counselor and the other girls in her group about her wish to be a boy which had been stirred up by playing the part of Joan, who pretended to be a boy to save her country. She spoke of her jealousy of her brothers, and her feeling that if she had been a boy, her family might have loved her more.

I had always been fascinated by Joan of Arc, and I had been a tomboy, wearing my brother's outgrown overalls long before it had been fashionable. I was amazed at the self-knowledge the counselor and the girls showed, and at their willingness to talk openly about how they felt. I wanted this understanding for myself. I wanted to know who I was. But how could I salvage that initial interview?

"I think I couldn't talk to you yesterday, when you asked me about myself, because you remind me of my father," I told Bettelheim the next day. I didn't know if this was true, but it might be true. I was aware of the same intense wish to please him, wanting to distinguish myself with a brilliant insight or a perfectly constructed phrase, that I felt at home with my father at the dinner table. I also knew that this was my only hope of saving the job, which I now wanted. Depth of understanding was the key here. I didn't have it, but I knew somehow that this was the way to begin.

I got the job.

CHAPTER 8

He Knows I Know He Knows

I keep thinking of Jason, in the older class, telling me that while his obsession with violence lasted he thought everything that didn't have to do with blasting someone's guts out was boring. Could Jason help me understand why some of my children love this violent play?

I see him in the hall one morning and ask if he would talk with me more about violence in play. His willingness surprises me. He quickly figures out a time when my class's recess intersects with a period his teacher might allow him to miss, and he is waiting for me at the appointed time. He sits on the edge of the small round table in my room while I sit on a small chair.

"Would you tell me more about your interest in violence?" I ask him.

"You sort of have to wait," he begins. "Last year, my parents and my teacher were worried about my obsession with vampires. That has passed and I got into violent computer games. Now computer games are fading away. It all started when I was little, with Power Ranger and Batman."

"Do you always have something violent on your mind?" I ask. As he talks, I'm trying to understand who it is who "sort of has to wait." Is it the adult who must be patient for the obsession to leave, or is it Jason who must wait for a new one to appear?

"I almost always have something," he answers. "It lasts for six months, or a year if I'm lucky."

"Do you *like* it to last longer?" I ask, still unclear.

"It's sort of annoying," he answers, "when you like something but you only sort of like it. It's sort of hard not to have something you really, really like."

"So you prefer it when you're obsessed with something?" I have trouble digesting this idea. I had assumed his obsession made life difficult for him, with parents and teachers placing limits on his violent interests, trying to convince him he should think about other things.

"Yeah." He leaves no room for doubt, now. "In school," he explains, "I can stop thinking about it and just do what I'm doing. In the car, when my mom is driving me to school, I think about violent games."

"Tell me what you like about being obsessed," I ask. "What's the good feeling?"

"Well, if there's something you really like, that you have exposure to, and it's sort of like you really, really like this book, and someone took it away from you, and you get it back and you just have to read it, it's like that."

Now I understand. The only thing better than being in the middle of a good book is discovering a new favorite author, knowing there are more books to explore when this one is done. And what about my love of writing? The best part is being in the middle of a writing project that's going well. Like Jason, I think about it in the car, planning what I'll work on in the evening, or when I get up the next morning. Is that how Seth feels about Deadman?

"Has your interest in violence ever caused you a problem?" I ask, wondering if the problem is exclusively in the eyes of the adults.

"This summer," he says, "I had a major obsession which is still sort of with me. All I could think about was video games. We went to Colorado and we were on the top of a mountain and it was so pretty, it was just the best place, and I spent the whole time reading my game magazine, and that's just like all violence. Well, it has a few strategy games.

"But I don't think my parents noticed. They'd say, 'Why don't you come outside?' and I'd say, 'I'm tired. My leg hurts,' and I'd lie on my bed and read.

"But I know violence is bad," he continues. "When I was little, if someone called me 'stupid,' I would hit him. But now, if they called me 'stupid,' I would laugh and walk away. I would say, 'If I was stupid, why would I have all these friends?' When you're a little kid, you're more impressionable. It sticks with you more. First, you have to know that violence is wrong. My parents don't let me play with toy guns. When I was little, my mom said, 'I'll buy you the action figures if you throw away the weapons.' And we have a TV, but we don't have cable, so we can only watch movies. Now I'm older, my dad is more comfortable with me seeing stuff like that, 'cause he knows I know it's wrong. And he knows I know he knows."

Maybe you have to be old enough to understand "he knows I know he knows" to be able to understand another person's point of view at the same time as keeping in mind your own, before you can enjoy violence and still know you will not act it out in real life.

CHAPTER 9

The F-word

"Last week, Aaron told me he learned the F-word," his mother whispers to me as we watch the children come into the classroom and settle into their morning activities. She has moved aside, so that her back is toward the children, and she nervously avoids my eyes. "I almost hit the roof," she continues, "but I tried to remember everything I've read about how to handle this, so I said, 'Oh?' and he said, 'Yeah, it's frow up.'"

We both laugh, but she continues, anxiously pushing her one loose strand of blond hair back into her tidy ponytail. "Then, this week, he came home with the real thing. I flipped out, and I told him that if he ever said that word again in my house, I'd wash his mouth out with soap." She smiles ruefully. "I wouldn't even know how to do it," she adds.

Even as she laughs, I know she's serious. In September, Aaron, just five, was as innocent as they come. He still played house instead of war. He said thank-you when I gave him his snack. He always let the new boy join his game. Now, after just a few months in my class, he's learned to swear and play shoot-'em-up games.

I know that at five, young boys often move away from their ties to their mothers and start to watch and copy the mannerisms of the bigger boys. Still, I am concerned that the violence and sex in the language of some of the children in the class might affect the younger children in the group.

I try to reassure Aaron's mother. "He loves to learn about letters and words," I tell her. "Last week, we listed words beginning with f. He must be fascinated by the idea that there's an f word that can't be spoken."

I think she is reassured, but I am not. I hate censorship. Yet this year, I find myself constantly censoring what the children say.

Two weeks later, walking by the art table, I hear the dirtiest ditty I have ever heard coming from the mouths of babes. Do they know what the words mean? If I make an issue of it, they will realize they've said something important, and it will be more likely to spread in secret. If I say nothing, I'm condoning it.

Aaron comes up to me nervously. "They're saying something not nice," he understates. In case I've missed it, he repeats the jingle, adding hand motions. Yes, he knows what it means.

Seth looks up from the picture he's drawing of torpedoes blowing up a battleship. "That's gross," he says. "Only someone who was gay would like that."

Great. Now in addition to violent play and smut, I have to deal with lack of respect for gays and lesbians. I remind myself that all the teachers made a commitment this year to deal with homophobia. I had decided that rather than bring in books on the subject, I would deal with the issue when it came up in class. Now it has, and I can't think of a thing to say. Clearly, these kids are too sophisticated for simplified answers and will ask some heavy questions if I bring it up for discussion. I am not prepared. I tell myself I need time to think about the problem.

I'm the type who's embarrassed by dirty jokes. I never discussed sex with friends in high school. I got the little knowledge I had from the library, where I had a job shelving books for fifty cents an hour. As I put the books away, I thumbed through each likely possibility, looking for the information I wanted. I got fired for working too slowly.

I am not eager to tell a bunch of children who are five and six but who speak like adolescents, whose parents don't want them discussing sex, why gay men are no more likely to enjoy a dirty rhyme than anyone else. I certainly will not do it when my student teacher, visiting parents, or other adults are in the room.

What am I afraid of? Not that the children will get out of control. I've been teaching over twenty years, and I know how to run an orderly discussion. I must be afraid I'll be asked a question I'm not prepared to answer, one that I find embarrassing. I might feel my neck and face turn red in front of these young children.

Finally, a day arrives when no outsiders are in the room and I have no more excuses.

"The other day," I begin at morning meeting, "someone was singing a little song."

"What song?" Alison asks.

"I don't even know it and I don't want to know what it was." I look at Alison's puzzled face and realize that what I have said makes no sense to her.

"It had a lot of bathroom talk in it," I explain. She nods. Now she understands what I'm getting at. I continue. "A child who was listening to the song said, 'That's gross. Only somebody who was gay would like that.'"

"What is 'gay'?" Alison asks.

Nina explains. "One use is when two men love each other."

"Nina's right," I confirm. "When two men love each other and want to live together, they can call themselves 'gay.' That doesn't mean they like gross songs. It just means they love someone who's the same gender. 'Gender' means a man or a woman."

"Get married?" Seth gets to the next point directly.

"They might want to get married," I hedge.

"I'm not getting married!" Seth announces. The sex of his proposed spouse is not the important issue here, it seems.

"I saw this movie about gay men," Nina says. "They all act silly."

"Some people think that gay men act silly," I tell her. "In some movies, they make fun of people who are gay, but in real life you might know some people who are gay and not even realize it, because they act like everyone else." I wonder if they've noticed that Linda, in the class next door, has two moms.

But Seth brings us back to Nina's movie. "I saw that movie," he says. "It was a real-life show."

"It was probably pretend," I tell him. "People were acting out a story, just the way we act out the stories you write at writers' workshop, and sometimes you act silly, too."

"Why are they making fun of them?" Alison asks.

"Some people make fun of people who are different than they are," I say.

"Excuse me," Joel interrupts. "They can't have children, right?"

"Only moms can have babies," I agree. "But sometimes men who are gay want to have a family and they adopt a child."

"What do you mean 'adopt'?" Alison continues in her role of demanding clarity.

"I have friends," I say, "a man and a woman. They wished and wished for a baby, but they didn't have one. They found out that there was a woman who was going to have a baby but she knew she would not be able to take good care of her child. My friends adopted that baby and they take care of it, and they love it just like any other parents."

"Well, I'm adopted," Joel says, "and that's what my mom told me."

The children look at him in astonishment. They have known him since September and never realized he had an exciting past.

"Did you go to one of those places for babies who don't have parents?" Nina asks.

"No," Joel says, looking puzzled.

"Some babies are adopted right after they're born," I explain. "But if there's no home for a baby that needs one, it can go to one of those homes until they find one."

"Was I adopted?" Seth asks me. I become aware of how serious he has been through this whole discussion, not trying to interrupt with clowning as he sometimes tries to do.

"I don't know," I answer him. "You have to ask your mom and dad about that."

"I'm not adopted," Alison says. "I have pictures of when I was born."

Despite their movie-watching sophistication, these children

are not really so different from the children I have taught in the past. They have learned to repeat the words they hear from the media, with its explicit language of sex and violence, even when they do not understand what the words mean. When our discussion unravels this confusion, they are able to express the same questions that young children have always asked. They want to know who they really are, and if their parents love them.

I remember imagining that I was adopted, to explain what I saw at the time as the preferential treatment my mother gave to my brother. I pretended that in reality I was of royal blood. Like King Arthur, my true identity would soon be revealed.

These young children learn the F-word too young, while I learned it mortifyingly late. They have too much information, while I did not have enough. But perhaps the solution is the same, and we can learn from each other, growing from the opportunity to talk openly, to ask questions and express our concerns, without fear or embarrassment.

CHAPTER 10

Anaconda

I have been looking for a chance to talk with Seth alone, casually. This does not happen easily, since he is usually with Daniel from the moment he comes in. Or perhaps I'm reluctant, finding excuses. I don't really want to talk with Seth about violence and sex.

But one morning, seeing him alone at a table drawing, I sit down near him, but not too near. I am careful to give us both some room. While I watch him add red dots to the character lying on the ground, I wonder what to ask him. Do I really want to know what is under his skin, to see the world through the eyes of a boy who loves violence?

"Did you see a movie that was too scary or gross?" I ask him.

"*Anaconda*," he answers immediately. "It was about people being swallowed up by a giant snake. It swallows the bad guy, spits him out, and he dies. Then a guy and a girl die, and there's only three people left on the boat."

I had expected more bravado. I thought Seth would be reluctant to admit to being scared, and I am surprised at how eager he is to talk.

"What was the goriest part?" I ask, gathering courage to hear.

"Well, the guy that got aten got spit out, and there was acids on him."

I am appalled that he has seen such explicit gore. At the same time, I am relieved that I could ask and that he could talk about it so easily. I decide to take the next step. "I noticed you've been talking about sex a lot lately," I say. "Was there anything sexy you've seen?"

"They weren't having sex," he answers, adding one more red spot to the figure on his page.

Do six-year-olds today know about "having sex"?

"But a boy and a girl in *Anaconda* were kissing," he continues. "It was gross. It was just *supposed* to be about a giant anaconda killing everybody."

I can remember when a couple kissing was more disgusting than a giant anaconda spitting out dead people.

"Anything else?" I ask.

"People having sex on TV," he says, staring at his drawing.

I would like to protect him from these images that he is too young to handle. "You know how the fighting you see on TV and in the movies isn't like real fighting?" I tell him. He nods. "Well, it's the same thing with sex. Sex is about how babies are made, how your life began. But when they show it in movies, it's just as fake as a giant anaconda eating people up. They want to make it look gross or exciting or scary so people will go to see it. But if you want to know how babies really are made, ask your mom." I make a mental note to call her, so she has a chance to prepare for this.

"It seems to me," I continue, "that all this violence and sex is keeping you from concentrating in school. It's like you can't get it out of your mind."

"I can't," he agrees, " 'cause I watch TV all day."

I can't tell if this is real, or a form of bragging, or an excuse. But from my discussion with the older kids, I know how hard it is to resist this obsession. Certainly, it is more than a six-year-old can do alone.

"Maybe for your birthday, you could ask for a few of those boxes of one thousand Popsicle sticks and a glue gun," I suggest. He nods.

For the next few days, he goes out of his way to sit next to me, even leaning against me, and he doesn't pull back when I put my arm around his shoulder. Maybe I can protect him, after all.

————

"I was walking around," Nate tells me early one morning, "and these six-year-olds were talking about R-rated movies. And they're movies that I don't even watch. Are there any kids who watch scary movies in here?"

"I have some kids who say they've seen *Anaconda*," I tell him.

"Whew!" he says. "I don't even have any desire to see these two snakes just terrorize these people. A shoot-'em-up movie doesn't really scare me, but I get scared if it's realistic."

I remember my question "Did you see a movie that was too scary or gross?" that elicited such an honest response from Seth. Would an older boy be willing to talk about what scared him?

"Did you ever watch anything that seemed so scary you were a little bit sorry you had seen it?" I ask carefully.

"Oh yeah," he answers, sitting down on the small table next to my stack of the children's dictated stories. "I've seen a lot of movies I was kind of sorry about. I saw one where a guy takes pictures and he's like watching from his rear window and the bad guy goes after him. The guy's totally disabled: he's in a wheelchair, so he can't get out and run. I was so scared! I finally got over it, but it was a very scary movie."

"Is there anything that helps you when you see something that's too scary?" I ask.

"What's really scary," he tells me, "is the movies that *can* happen. What I do is, I say, 'It's just a movie,' and I get over it, after a time. . . . I saw this Halloween story," he continues, "with all kinds of gruesome stuff. The pictures were entering my head, guys pop up at the window. Parents have to be careful, what they let kids see," he warns me.

"In my class," I tell him, "it seems as though some kids can't get the violence out of their minds. When we do math or writing workshop, they're still thinking about it. Does that happen to you?"

"Sometimes I think about a movie I've seen when I'm very bored, especially if the teacher is talking a long time and I'm not interested in it. But then she says, 'Nate, what did I just say?' and you're like, 'Uh-oh. Ah, the square root of four is um . . . .' She can tell when you're thinking about something else."

"I remember getting a gold star next to my name because I was looking as though I was listening to the teacher, while I was really imagining I was riding my palomino horse across the plains," I tell him.

"I don't pay attention if she's talking about something I already know," Nate says. "If I miss something important, I can ask my friends. But if I need to listen to the teacher, I can put the other stuff out of my mind and not think about it."

"Maybe the kids in my class haven't learned to do that yet," I say.

"Yeah, we're older," Nate answers. "We know how to disguise it better."

They can disguise it better, and they tell me that they can deal with the violence they see, but I still wonder if it affects them more than they realize or admit.

CHAPTER 11

Vulnerable Bad Guys, Electric Fences, and Poisonous Snakes

At lunch, I am sitting at a small table with Seth, Daniel, and Alison. This is not a naturally occurring seating arrangement in this group. The almost total segregation of sexes that occurred when the children chose their own tables had led to a large, raucous group of boys, shouting across to one another, falling off chairs, and laughing too loudly. I arranged mixed groups, two boys and two girls at each table, but since the second girl at Alison's table is out sick, I am hesitant to leave her, as I imagine, to the wolves. I sit down to join and protect her.

"This turns into a battleship," Seth tells Daniel, pointing to the cardboard box and Popsicle stick structure at his feet. "We can tell 'em it turns into a battleship, we just can't show 'em *how* it turns into a battleship."

Alison puts down her yogurt, pushes her brown bangs out of her eyes, and looks at me. "Why do they like violence so much?" she asks.

Seth and Daniel continue, uninterrupted, while Alison and I discuss them. "I imagine," I tell her, "that it's like being the bad baby in a game of house."

She frowns, puzzled.

"Do you sometimes like to pretend to be the baby that misbehaves?" I ask. "The one who cries, throws the food, won't do what the mama says?"

She smiles, beginning to understand. I continue. "It can be fun to pretend to do things that are too bad to do in real life."

She nods and we listen some more. Then Seth says something so softly that at first I think I've misheard.

"I have a problem," he seems to be telling his lunch box. "Joel makes things better than me. His battleship is better."

Daniel answers. "Just say to yourself, 'Oh, those are the same as mine.' Then you won't mind."

But Seth is not reassured. "Joel's just look better."

"Is it important that you make the best?" I ask.

Seth does not answer. Instead, he turns to Daniel. "Do you have any toothpicks?" he asks. "Well, we could glue them together and it will be a barbed-wire fence so it will go zzt, zzt! When you plug in something to the electric outlet, the wires that are across the room will start to electrocute people when they touch it."

Or when they ask too many questions? I wonder. Or when their art project turns out too well?

Daniel immediately joins the fantasy. "Want to know something? I want you to give me two hundred blue wires, ten black wires, and nine orange wires. And then, give me two battery packs. Make it go up to twenty bolts!"

Seth approves. "You electrocute them so much that they'll die? You just say, 'Zzt, zzzt! uh!'"

"Good," Daniel says. At first I think he's agreeing with Seth's execution of the invisible enemy, but as he takes a cup of chocolate pudding out of his lunch box, I realize my mistake. "Good. My mom remembered to pack me a spoon!" he says as he begins to eat his dessert.

The image of their electric fence hits me like an imaginary lightning bolt. Could the boys' violent fantasies defend them from vulnerability? Does this twenty-bolt fence protect as well as kill? I am so preoccupied with this idea, I almost miss the next installment.

"Everything in my lunch, I don't like," Seth says sadly, looking in his box.

"I could help you make a list of food you'd like your mom to give you," I suggest, thinking of the opportunity for getting him to use his newly acquired writing skills for important communication. But Seth has found something that cheers him more than my list. He reaches into his lunch box and pulls out a rubber snake.

"This glows in the dark," he tells Daniel. "My mom says that when my frog dies, I can get a snake for a pet!" He pauses. "Last night I put this down and my mom went to sleep and when she woke up, she screamed, 'Eeeee!'"

"Put that away, please," I say firmly. "You can use it when you go out to recess." I will not be the imaginary mother who loses control.

"This is a yellow-bellied water snake," Seth tells Daniel, as he replaces it in his lunch box. "It eats rodents and it will poison a person."

I look at Alison, who is listening carefully. What would a girl do in the face of a disappointing lunch? I wonder. She might push her lunch box across the table and burst into tears. Or she might go to the dress-up clothes and turn herself into an imperious queen or a naughty baby. I used to pretend to be Annie Oakley, singing, "Anything you can do, I can do better!" at the top of my voice, so my older brother would be sure to hear.

I think back to how quickly I demanded that Seth put his rubber snake away. The fantasies of the boys feel more threatening to me than those of the girls, but could it be that electric fences and poisonous snakes give them the same protection from vulnerability that I once found behind my old wing chair?

CHAPTER 12

A Vulnerable Writer

"Seth," I say as we gather for morning meeting the next day, "Could we talk about the problem with your battleship?"

"You mean, about Joel's being better?" he asks. I nod. "You can tell them," he answers.

When the children have gathered, I explain. "Seth says he feels bad because he thinks Joel makes better battleships than he does," I tell them.

"Seth!" Travis exclaims. "How I make my stuff, is that I try to copy you, 'cause you make such good stuff!"

Gregory confirms this. "When I saw Travis's ship, I recognized Seth's."

"Seth," Alison tells him firmly. "Don't worry about it, just keep on working on your thing. It doesn't matter if Joel's is better than yours. It just matters that you like it."

"That's just what I realized last night," I tell Alison, "when I read my story at my writing group." The intense hush settles in the room that always occurs when I tell the children about my life outside of school.

"What writing group?" Alison asks.

"Once a month, I go to a kind of writing workshop for adults," I explain. "We each bring something to read, and everyone gives suggestions.

"Last night, I brought a story I had written that I liked and I was very eager to read. I was a little worried, because I didn't know what the other writers would think. I came in late, and sat down next to a new poet who was just starting to read. She had a whole briefcase of poems, and even a whole published book of her work on the table."

In my mind, I picture the scene: the poet, her organized portfolio, her confident manner. I am most intimidated by the poets, with their tight phrases and multifaceted images. When she started to read, I knew immediately that she was out of my class. How could I read my dumb story? But sitting at the table next to her, my turn would be next. I remembered Seth's twenty-bolt fence, and wished I could find comfort in its protection.

"I felt so nervous," I explain to the children, "I didn't want to read my story anymore. But I made myself do it."

"What happened?" Nina asks. "Did they like it?"

"Everyone was very quiet while I was reading," I answer. "When I was done, one writer said, 'This is fascinating!' The new poet said, 'I think you should send it out to *The New Yorker*.' That's a magazine for adults," I explain. "They had some good suggestions for making it better, too." The children smile at my success.

"After that happened," I say, "I realized it was silly of me to try to compare my story to her poem." Sometimes it's hard to remember what Alison told us, "It just matters that you like it."

CHAPTER 13

Strangled

"So. You vere afraid your father vould strangle you, eh?"

I looked up at Dr. B. in surprise. He had walked into the staff room silently while I sat on a couch, drinking my coffee. He always wore quiet, rubber-soled shoes, allowing him to seem to materialize in a ghostly way. I looked up at him, only because I was sitting and he was standing. His presence was so imposing, it took me about two years to realize that I was taller than he was.

"You vere afraid he vould strangle you. That is vhy you do not let anyone touch your neck!"

My neck? What was he talking about? Then I remembered. One of the children had come up behind me, and she had startled me by playfully putting her hands around my neck. I had shouted at her to let go. I never let anyone touch my neck. It made me feel as though I was being strangled.

That's not even true, about my father, I thought. He never lifted a finger to hurt me. I was afraid only of his angry silences, which could last for days, or even weeks. But they were never directed at me. I was his favorite.

This time, Dr. B. had it all wrong.

CHAPTER 14

The Rules of Violence

I receive a concerned phone call from Gregory's mother about the games the children are playing at recess. At our next morning meeting, I tell the children, "Some of you have told your parents that other children are talking at recess about things that are too gross or scary. Can you tell us what it is that you don't want to hear, so we can ask everyone not to talk about it?" I wonder whether any of them will admit publicly to this concern.

Gregory speaks immediately. "I know," he says. "I told my mom because I didn't like the game where people took eyeballs out."

I am relieved that Gregory spoke up first. If Seth had begun with a defense of violence, it might have been hard for others to admit their feelings. But Gregory is a leader, a frequent team captain in soccer, and Nina's best friend. Once they have heard him speak, most of the children will feel they can talk honestly.

"When we play Super Mario Brothers," Travis says, "the princess is turned to guck. I don't like to play that game."

"I think that taking eyeballs out and slime are both gross," Alison agrees. "And I don't like it when people chop you in half and get you all bloody."

I am startled by the image her pronoun implies: I did not imagine one of the children being chopped and bloody. I had pictured only an invisible enemy.

"But this is probably everything what's in violent stories!" Seth complains.

"No," I tell him. "You can still have good guys and bad guys getting killed without chopping them up and having them get all bloody."

Nina speaks for the first time. "I don't think people should say, 'I'm going to chop you up in my story if you don't do this part,'" she explains. Threats are another aspect of the game I had not thought about. I am glad to have Nina on my side.

"Nothing's too gross for me!" Seth boasts. I resist the urge to take him down a peg by reminding him of *Anaconda*. His trust thathe can tell me privately when he is frightened is more important.

"Taking off your socks and smelling them," Gregory says. "That's too gross!"

"I don't want people to take a sword and stick it through someone's tummy and bones fall out," Kathy adds.

Gregory looks at the growing list I've been writing on the board as the children talk. "Erase the socks," he tells me. "I want the socks."

"I don't want anyone chopping their whole head off," Daniel says. I am surprised to hear him taking a different side from Seth's, but then he continues, "They slice their head off, then their neck, then their legs, then their feet." Is this an excuse to gross us out? I decide to take him at his word, and add his examples to the list.

"These gross and scary things all fit into the rules we made earlier in the year about violence in the classroom," I point out. I write those rules down, too:

1. No excessive blood.
2. No chopping off of body parts.
3. No guts or other things that belong inside the body can come out.

"We can use the same rules out at recess that we use for the stories we act out in the classroom," I explain.

"But that's probably half the stuff that's in violence!" Seth protests again. "How 'bout us? That's no fair!"

"Children have to be in school," I tell him. "They need a safe place where they don't feel grossed out. If your parents let you, you can play what you want at your own house."

"Fine!" Seth answers defiantly. "I'll do it at my house! All day! With no one to tell me to stop!"

"Me too!" Gregory joins him, in spite of the fact that he had been the first to admit to disliking the explicit violence, and had agreed with our original rules. "I'll lock myself up in a room!" he adds, heightening the dramatic effect.

"Why can't we do it at recess, where if anybody says, 'I don't like that,' we just move to a different place where people don't mind?" Nina suggests.

Gregory adds to her proposal. "One recess we play no violence, and the next one we play violence."

I feel discouraged to see our near agreement slipping away. But Nina explains the rule she and Gregory are developing. "That way, the people who don't like violence, but they do want to play with the people who like gross stuff, can play with them next recess."

This seems so reasonable, I find it hard to disagree.

"V-O-A-T, V-O-A-T," Aaron spells. "Let's vote!" He has recently learned that when two vowels go walking, the first one does the talking.

I summarize the new proposal: Children can play games involving violent language at alternate recesses, so that children who do not like violence have a chance to play with their friends who do like it. If anyone objects to the violence, the players must find a new location. Of course, there is never any real hitting or pushing in the game. When they pretend to fight, they can never touch one another.

We vote. The children adopt the new rule. I feel as though I've lost. Maybe I should have made the rule myself, without allowing for a vote.

We came so close to a nearly unanimous banning of most explicit verbal violence at recess, before Nina and Gregory turned the tide against it. Why did they do that, when they so courageously spoke against the excessive violence at the beginning of the discussion? Surely they are not afraid of Seth's anger. I've seen them disagree with him publicly many times. Could it be that they want to protect children from hearing the violence they don't like, but they also want Seth to be allowed to play the games he loves? Their recess rules have ingeniously protected everyone, in a complex agreement I would never have imagined. They require the children playing together to listen to each other, to respect one another's needs, and to be inclusive, exactly the values I've stressed all year.

My respect for the children and for the group process goes up, the more I think about what has taken place. We have an agreement that is better than any rule I could have imposed.

Girls!

I am proud of our progress dealing with the issues of exclusion that seem to crop up around the children's violent fantasy play. But on conference day, I discover that the girls in the class are practicing their own more subtle form of exclusion.

Kayla's mother comes in first. "I don't know what to do about the car pool," Kayla's mother confides. "As soon as the girls get in the car to go to dance class, Kayla starts in on Anna. She'll say, 'That picture you made of "The Twelve Dancing Princesses" was so silly, Anna. They're supposed to wear fancy dresses, not pants!' Then Anna says, 'Kayla's not being nice,' and Kayla tells her, 'Why are you such a tattletale?'" Kayla's mother sighs, "I'm glad their dance class meets only once a week."

"What do you do about it?" I ask.

"We talk with her all the time about being nice," she answers, "but it doesn't seem to help."

"I haven't noticed a problem in school," I say. "I know Kayla always wants to be the fanciest princess or the oldest sister, but that's not unusual at five and six. Since Anna is one of the new girls this year, Kayla may be afraid she'll cause some unwelcome changes in the friendship groups. I'll keep an eye on them," I reassure her.

To my surprise, the next three mothers of girls who come in describe their daughters' concern about the way Kayla treat

Anna. They tell me that their girls feel uncomfortable when Kayla compliments them and deliberately leaves Anna out of the conversation. How have I missed this subtle but systematic exclusion?

Why Anna? To my teacher's eye, Anna is a kind and thoughtful girl who is unlikely to have started the conflict.

She does have one problem. Anna is afraid of blood. She is, therefore, afraid of falling down and scraping her knees, so she avoids all active play. In September, she didn't want to go to the playground at recess, but I convinced her to take her doll to the picnic table. Once when she did fall, a tiny drop of blood squeezed out from the dirt on her hand and she screamed, "I'm bleeding! I'm bleeding!" before she even had a good look at it.

Recently, her friends have started to bring their dolls to play with her at the table. Last week I saw them run across the playground to push their young charges on the swings. Anna stumbled and fell, and I saw the fleeting look of panic pass over her face. But she got up, brushed off her knee, and ran to catch up with her friends.

Kayla, on the other hand, rarely cries. She's used to playing with her older brothers and with their friends. When she's not pretending to be the oldest princess, she's on the soccer field, taking rough-and-tumble play without a whimper. I suspect she has little patience for Anna's obvious weakness.

The parents' complaints remind me of an incident I had forgotten. Last week, I saw Kayla put red paint on her hand while she was painting at the art table, and then show it to Anna, pretending it was blood. "Just kidding," she said quickly when she saw I was watching. I am reminded of Seth's aside to Kayla, "I can't wait to tease Daniel 'cause he has a Little Mermaid game."

For two days I watch the girls, noticing, for the first time, Kayla's subtle criticism and exclusion of Anna. "I like your dress, Kathy," she says. "And those are beautiful shoes, Alison." She pauses, and I can feel the tension, as everyone waits to see if she will compliment Anna, the only other girl in the group. Kayla looks toward me, sees I am watching, and adds, "And you have a pretty headband, Anna." I notice Kayla disagrees with every idea Anna suggests, but disagreeing is not prohibited in my class. I can never quite nail down what she has done wrong, so that I can talk with her about it.

I have no tolerance for Kayla's sneaky exclusion. I want her mother to tell Kayla that she won't take her to dance class if she is mean to Anna in the car pool. With satisfaction, I imagine her dropping Anna at the class and taking Kayla home to sulk. I want to tell Kayla that she can't use paints at the art table if she's going to use them to frighten Anna. I relish the thought of seeing Kayla as the outcast that she tries to make Anna.

Surprised at my own venom, I realize that such a punitive stance will only drive the problem further underground, while what I need to do is to bring it out where we can talk about it.

In fourth grade, I was the new girl and the outsider. Before lunch each day, one child in the class said grace. Miss McNunlty, the teacher, began with the first child in the first row, and proceeded toward the back, before moving on to the second row. I was in the second seat of the third row, because I had trouble seeing the blackboard. By the time she got to the end of the second row, I began to seriously worry. The blessings I knew were in Hebrew. "*Boruch atah Adonai.*" I imagined reciting the prayer before lunch to the snickers of the other children.

I didn't tell my mother about my problem. I was afraid she would feel hurt that I was embarrassed by our prayers. Jews had risked their lives for centuries to say prayers in their own way. How could I be such a coward?

Maybe I could copy one of the prayers the other children recited. "God is great. God is good. Now I thank him for our food. Amen." Three lines, and so easy! But I was pretty sure he could strike me dead, right there at the Prince School, for pretending to be Christian.

I imagined myself reciting the Christian prayer by day, secretly lighting the Sabbath candles at night, like the Jews during the

Spanish Inquisition. They were threatened with death for saying Jewish prayers, so they prayed at night, hidden in cellars with trapdoors. Were the snickers of fourth graders equivalent to death threats? I didn't think God would see it that way.

The day before it was my turn, in desperation I told my mother. She translated the Hebrew blessing into English: "Blessed art thou, O Lord, our God. . . ." How I longed for the three simple lines of Christian grace.

At lunchtime, I mumbled my words quickly, hoping no one would hear, the English translation sounding strange to my ears.

On the playground at recess, a girl named Shirley shouted, "The Jews killed Jesus!"

"That's a lie!" I called back.

"They did so! The nuns told us!" she answered.

Shirley had the waist-length, red curly hair I always wanted, and she was popular. I felt my neck turn red. Angry and confused, my mind ran through my Jewish history book, but there was no information about Jesus to enlighten me. Could the Jews have killed Jesus? I pictured the life-size statue of the baby Jesus in the manger in the Public Garden at Christmas. I went out of my way to see the crèche on my way to school. I loved the wise men leading their camels and bearing gifts for the child. Why would the Jews have murdered him?

Then I remembered the chapter on the Inquisition. Weren't the Jews accused of drinking children's blood on Passover? Could the nuns be teaching those lies today? Maybe Shirley made it all up.

My religion isolated me, as Anna's fears make her vulnerable to Kayla's teasing. I don't want my old wounds to stop me from seeing what is happing in my classroom. I am ready to look at the girls, and see what I am missing.

I don't have to wait long. Shortly after school begins one morning, Anna comes up to me, her bottom lip pushed out in a pout. "It's not fair!" she says in a voice that threatens to become tearful. "Kayla picked up a round key. She said, 'Oh, look! This is the magic key we were looking for!'" As she speaks, Anna twirls the ends of her hair around her finger, making a knot.

Kayla interrupts quickly. "But, Anna! Look at all those keys! How 'bout you have those three and I'll have these three!"

Anna looks at me, still pouting. "But then Kayla gets the round one."

Nina, building with blocks nearby, is listening in on their conversation. "I think they should both find the same key with the same letters on them. Then they'll be happy," she explains.

"I have an idea," Anna says. "How about there's no magic key and then it will all be fair."

"But isn't Nina's idea fair?" I ask. The writer in me wants Kayla to be allowed to weave her story of the magic key. "Kayla wants to pretend there's a magic key. That's part of the story she's telling in her game."

"I know!" Kayla says. "How about no one uses the round key and we each have three of the others?" She is surprisingly willing to give up the single round key rather than give up the idea of the magic key.

"No!" Anna comes in quickly. "I just think if Kayla had three keys she might lose one. And if I found it, she'd get mad at me and then I'd be sad because I don't like it when she yells at me."

"That wouldn't happen," Kayla tells her. "Let's just use keys, okay?"

I am surprised to find myself siding with Kayla. What if I couldn't write the book I wanted because everyone couldn't write it? Anna's whining and threatening to cry if she can't control the game annoys me just as it must annoy Kayla, and it reminds me of Seth's controlling his imaginary party. I see Kayla calling Anna a tattletale in a new light.

"What do you think?" I ask the group of children in the nearby block area.

"Well, how many keys are there?" Gregory asks. "If there are four, they could each have two."

"We could write their names on a piece of paper," Patrick adds. "Each key could have a name on it, Kayla or Anna."

"I think they should make their own magic keys at the art table," Alison suggests.

Kayla suggests a new compromise. "I think Anna should have all the other keys and I only have this one round one." I am surprised again at how far she is willing to compromise.

"No," Anna says again. "No keys."

"Is it fair for Anna to say there shouldn't be any keys at all?" I ask, assuming I know the answer.

But Kathy startles me. "I think no one should play pretend," she says.

Alison speaks again. "I think that since Kathy and me and Kayla and Anna might come in and want a key, there might not be enough, so I think no one should have a key."

"I think we should buy enough keys for the whole class," Gregory suggests.

"My bear, Misty, could have the keys," Kayla suggests.

"No keys at all!" Seth says. "No keys! No keys!" I suspect he wants the discussion to end so his friends can get back to their block building.

"Maybe we should just play a different game," Kayla says quietly.

"I agree with Kayla," Anna says quickly.

"That's a good idea," adds Kathy.

I am disappointed. I didn't want Kayla to give up her idea of the magic key.

I wonder why I have never seen their relationship this way before. It is so easy to let my own identification with the excluded one blind me, so that I assume I know what is happening, rather than watching what is in front of my eyes.

On my drive home, I make a decision. Remembering Gregory's advice, I stop at a hardware store and buy six of the shiniest, round, identical keys I can find.

The next morning, I present them to the class.

"They're gold!" the children exclaim eagerly.

After our meeting, the girls go to the dramatic play area, where they have already begun planning their next project, the *Nutcracker* ballet, leaving the six golden keys behind.

Once I begin watching for issues of exclusion, I seem to see them everywhere. I remember that in one of my conversations with Jason from the older class, he mentioned a child who was excluded. That child, Jason said, became fascinated with violence. Now I know I need him to tell me more about it. I invite him to talk with me again, and I ask him to tell me how he sees the connection between violence and exclusion.

"If someone doesn't have a friend," he begins, "and they want someone popular to be their friend, they start following that person around and being nice to him. That can be really annoying, so the popular kid tells him, 'Leave me alone.' "

This sounds so much like Joel and Seth, he might have been watching them.

Jason continues, "And the other kid gets his feelings hurt and starts following him around to annoy him. And the popular kid starts calling him names and goes off with his other friends."

Jason makes fleeting eye contact with me and then concentrates his attention on scratching off a blob of glitter glue stuck on the table. "If you're fighting with someone who has a lot of friends," he says, "you can't win. You just can't. I've had that experience before. If I'm mad at someone, and they call me names, I run at them and they dodge me and then all the kids start laughing and I just get madder. I mean, I've seen it happen to a lot of kids and it's happened to me, so I know what it's like.

"I also know what it's like to have a kid follow you around. There's a kid who wants me as a friend, but the way he wants my constant attention is really hard. I don't tell him to stop, 'cause he gets his feelings easily hurt. I kind of know. I've been on both sides."

How I wish Joel had chosen someone like Jason to follow around!

"If you're a kid who's following someone around," Jason says, "when they're with their friends, you have to let them be. And when they're by themselves, you have to know when to talk. You have to see it from both sides."

Would Jason have learned such wisdom from following around a kinder child? Or is it necessary to be hurt to learn these skills?

When we began our study of violence in play, I did not expect to study exclusion. The frequency with which the subject came up has taken me by surprise.

Although I still have questions about the nature of the connection between violence and exclusion, I am increasingly convinced that the tie exists. The act of exclusion, as Jason describes it, can lead to a cycle of violence. In addition, the intensity of the pain of the excluded child makes me believe the act of exclusion may be a violent action in itself.

The girls' exclusion is quieter than that of the boys' noisy quarrels. If I don't hear the comment and see the context, I may never know it has happened. Even if I do hear it, the incident can be so subtle it is hard to pin down. Yet quiet exclusion may be just as painful, and since it is harder to name, the victim can find it more difficult to lodge a complaint. The resulting injury to the excluded girl's self-image may be more difficult to see but it may not be easier to heal.

CHAPTER 16

The White Ninja

Nina is a creative and imaginative storyteller. She loves action, but also knows how to bring it to a climax and a conclusion. When we act out the morning's dictated stories and the stories from our afternoon writing workshop, hers are a favorite, with both boys and girls eager to take a role.

So in the morning, when I see she has signed up on the list of children waiting to dictate a story to act out, I am eager to hear her next adventure.

"It's called 'The White Ninja,'" she begins, sitting down next to me at the round table. "The White Ninja chops the Blue Ninja in half. Hi-ah!" She makes the appropriate chopping motion with her hands as she speaks.

"But, Nina," I interrupt. "I'll write that down for you, but I don't think we can act it out. Doesn't it go against our rule for violence?" I look at her puzzled face. "The rule about blood," I explain, "and the one about guts."

Gregory has come over to the table to hear Nina's story. "I think it's okay if no blood went gushing out," he tells me.

Aaron is at the table drawing, waiting for his turn to tell a story. "I agree with Gregory," he tells me. "There's no guts, either."

They appear to be serious; they're not trying to put something over on me. Could it be they imagine a Ninja being sliced in half the way I picture cutting a gummy bear in two pieces?

"We'll talk about it at meeting," I promise. I'll have to see if anyone thinks it's too gross to act out.

Nina continues her story. "I'm the White Ninja," she explains. "The witch came swooping down to kill the White Ninja. But the White Ninja dodged the witch's powers. And the White Ninja said, 'That was a close one.' Then, while the White Ninja wasn't paying attention, the witch swooped down and grabbed the White Ninja, and the White Ninja took out his sword and put it up to scare the witch and the witch went, 'Ahh!' and she was frightened, so she let go of the White Ninja."

"I want to be the other Ninja," Gregory says. "The one that gets cut in half."

At meeting, I explain the problem. I suggest that if no one objects, we can act out the story, being aware of how it feels to be in the story as well as to watch it.

Everyone enjoys Nina's adventure, including Gregory, who gets cleanly sliced in half, with no blood and no guts.

CHAPTER 17

The Shooting Game

I walk out to the playground as recess is ending, planning to keep my class out for a few extra precious minutes of December sunshine. I walk around the colorful pile of winter jackets, carelessly discarded on the steps in the rare winter warmth.

"How's it going?" I ask Sylvia, the teacher on recess duty. Most days, lately, I come out to hear a catalog of complaints about my children, which includes their arguments about the rules of the shooting game, their latest outdoor invention.

"They've been okay," Sylvia tells me. "But I don't feel comfortable with all the shooting they've been doing."

My heart sinks. "Have they been fighting?" I ask. "We spent a long time this morning working out an agreement about the rules."

"No," Sylvia tells me. "I'm just uncomfortable with all the shooting. Can't they find something better to do? I think we should talk about this at staff meeting."

Bang. I point an invisible finger at her and shoot silently. But I have another kind of weapon. I try to articulate an answer that will convince her of the importance of the game. "If I prohibit the shooting game, they'll just lie and tell me they're pointing fire hoses instead of guns. But if I can help them make rules for respecting each other and playing the game safely, they will have a tool they can use anywhere, whether teachers are watching or not."

I decide to take an aggressive tack, heading off potential trouble. At the staff meeting that afternoon, I make an announcement. "My class is working hard on the rules of a shooting game they've been playing. We have discussed what is the fairest way to behave when they are 'shot,' and how long they must lie down after the shooter holds up a finger and says, 'Bang.'

"They've agreed to use only fingers for guns, to stay over an arm's length away when they 'shoot,' and to fall down and count to ten before getting up again when someone says, 'I got you.' Please let me know if they have problems following their own rules."

"I think we need to talk about shooting games at recess," Sylvia says. "Is it the best use of the children's time?"

The principal agrees to put the subject on a future agenda. I know how many issues are on her list already, and I relax, knowing it may never come up at all.

I wake up at two in the morning, replaying the conversation with Sylvia, letting my anger at her build, thinking of better answers I could have given. The children have learned so much about listening to one another, and about seeing different sides of an issue. Seth doesn't like to fall down "dead" when he is shot, but he knows that if he doesn't, Daniel will not want to "die" when Seth shoots him. Daniel knows that if he pretends he didn't hear Joel say, "I got you," his friends will call him on it and tell him he's cheating. How can Sylvia say so glibly, "Don't they have something better to do?"

But wait. I don't like the shooting game, either. I also wish they had something "better" to do. Nostalgically, I envision a class of four-year-olds playing in the sandbox, covered with mud and water, their arguments the simpler ones of sharing shovels and buckets, and I long for the innocent play of the days when I used to teach nursery school.

I hate the shooting game. That's why I'm so angry at Sylvia. I share her feelings, but I know now that I must listen to the arguments and help the children solve their problems, so that when these boys are on the far side of the playground, in their backyards or neighborhoods, they will know how to play the shooting game with fairness and respect.

I get out of bed and search through my bookshelf. I know Bettelheim wrote an article on child's play and parental disapproval. I find what I am looking for in an *Atlantic Monthly* magazine, March 1987. In talking about pretend shooting play, Bettelheim writes,

> Some parents even fear that such play may make a future killer of the child who thoroughly enjoys it, but the pitfalls of such thinking are many and serious.
>
> First, as playing with blocks does not indicate that a child will grow up to be an architect . . . so playing with toy guns tells nothing about what a child will do and be later in life. Second, one may reasonably expect that if through gun play a child feels that he can protect himself, and if he discharges many of his aggressive tendencies, then fewer of these will accumulate and require dangerous ways of discharge in later life. . . . Third, and by far the most important attitude, is parental fear that the child may become a violent person. This thought is far more damaging to the child's emotional well-being and his sense of self-worth than any play with guns can possibly be. If they seem to hold such a low opinion of him, it is apt to make him very angry at them and the world, and this increases his propensity to act out his anger . . . once he has outgrown parental control. (page 35)

Now I can go back to sleep. If the subject does come up in staff meeting, I'll have my own ammunition ready.

CHAPTER 18

Hippo and Baboon

My niece Rebecca, a college sophomore, has just returned from Zimbabwe when she comes to visit me. "These are pictures from the school for physically handicapped children where I worked," she tells me.

"This is Simba," she says, and I look into the smiling face of a child on his back on the floor. "He couldn't move from a lying-down position, so he was mostly on his stomach or back. He used his hands to roll where he wanted to go."

"Did he often smile like that?" I ask.

"Whenever I saw him, he had that happy, glowing smile," Rebecca says. "When I came, he would say, 'How are you. Fine.' His speech was slurred, and that was the only English he knew, but he seemed to have a positive attitude about everything. He would roll into the room, say something funny in Shona, his language, and everyone in the room would laugh.

"This is Luckmore," Rebecca says. She looks at my puzzled face. "Children often have names that are random English words." Rebecca shows me the next picture. "He couldn't use his hands, he couldn't talk, and his hips didn't work right, so he sat up on his butt and inched his way around with his hips." I look at Luckmore's beaming smile. "He could draw and write and pick things up with his toes. Once, while I was sitting with him, he picked up some small toys with his toes and put them in my pocket so gently, I didn't realize he'd done it! But he would often fall over and hit his head. He had huge bumps on his head because he couldn't balance very well." She tenderly touches the image of his head.

I think of the children in my class who think that happiness comes from a new Beanie Baby or a new bike, children who have so much but always want more.

"How can they be so happy?" I ask her.

"It struck me by surprise, too," she says. "I think that maybe when you have more, it takes more to get you to smile, because you're used to it. They have so little, when I paid attention to them, the smallest thing was an excuse to smile; any little game would get them glowing. If I went up to Simba, to talk with him or play a game, I'd get a huge smile."

I know that Rebecca's love has the power to make people happy. But I cannot picture those smiles on American children who have very little. I imagine them too busy wanting what they did not have.

Could we show the children in my class that happiness does not always come from getting a new movie or an expensive toy?

"Would you come to school with me tomorrow and show these pictures to my class?" I ask Rebecca. I sense her immediate nervousness. Confident conversing in several African languages with children whose immediate needs overwhelm me, she finds speaking in front of a group of young American children daunting. But she agrees to try.

I, too, am a bit nervous. Showing photographs of African children with severe physical disabilities is not a regular part of the curriculum. What will the children make of these smiling faces? Will they be bored? Or will they have nightmares?

The next day, Rebecca comes to school with me. I watch her at the art table helping Kathy make clothes for her Beanies, Rebecca's short-cropped dark hair bending over Kathy's blond curls. After she and the children seem comfortable together, I ask her to show the pictures.

They look at the picture of Luckmore, his toes curled in the air. "How does he move around?" Kathy asks, frowning at the photograph.

"He lies on the floor on his stomach and pushes himself with his feet," Rebecca answers. "He picks things up with his toes." We stare at his smiling face.

"What does he play with?" I ask.

"Scraps of food that fall on the floor, peelings from fruit," Rebecca tells us.

"He looks happy," Alison points out.

"Yes," Rebecca says. "I can't explain that, but these children seem to be very happy."

"Let's pretend we're children in Africa," I suggest. "We'll go outside to the sandbox and pretend we have only the sticks and stones that we found there. We won't use any of the plastic trucks or shovels."

"Can we use water from the fountain?" they ask. I start to say yes, but stop and look to Rebecca for guidance.

"If you were in the part of Africa where I worked," she explains, "you would have to carry all your water in a big pot from the river. You would never think of wasting it by pouring it on the dirt."

The children mill around the sandbox, unsure of what to do. Alison settles down first, making designs in the sand with sticks and stones. Aaron gathers twigs and starts to build a house. "Can we go in yet?" asks Seth. We don't stay out long. Most children don't find much to do.

We go inside and I read the children some African folk tales, to give them a view of this different culture. *Who's in Rabbit's House?*, a Masai tale retold by Verna Aardema, is their favorite. They love it when a tiny caterpillar hides in Rabbit's house and scares the larger animals by saying, "I am The Long One. I eat trees and trample on elephants," and they are delighted when Caterpillar is tricked into coming out by Frog, who pretends to be a poisonous snake.

Just before it is time to go home, we gather to act out the day's stories. Some were dictated to me in the morning. Others were written by the children during writing workshop.

"Rebecca," I ask, "would you tell a story for us to act out? One that an African child might tell?"

Again she hesitates, but again she agrees to try. "It's called 'Hippo and Baboon,' she begins. Seth acts the role of the hippo, Aaron is the baboon. They listen to her words and act out the story as she tells it. "Hippo and Baboon were best friends. And they lived together. So that meant that they had to do all the house chores together. They had to share. One of the chores was to go to the river and fetch water in a big pot and carry it on your head and bring it home. But Hippo was scared of the water."

Seth ad libs, "I don't want to go near the water. There's lions there."

Rebecca continues. "So Baboon didn't mind it. But he got sick of every day going to the river to fetch water and of carrying it back on his head. One day, Baboon said, 'I am not carrying up the water every day.' And since Hippo was scared of the water, he wouldn't carry any, so they didn't have any water. And they got so thirsty that they were both lying on the floor without being able to move and they were going to die of thirst. One day, Giraffe, who was their friend, came to see them, knocked on the door, and nobody answered.

"Knock, knock." Kathy enters the circle as Giraffe. Aaron groans and tries to lift his head a little.

"They didn't get up," Rebecca goes on. "She went into the house and saw Hippo and Baboon lying on the ground, almost dead. She said, "What's wrong? What's wrong?" Giraffe carried Hippo and Baboon to the river on her back. And she threw them into the river, both of them. And they wanted water so badly, Hippo forgot that he was scared of the water and they both drank and drank and drank and then they played in the water." The three children enjoy pretending to splash one another.

"And then Hippo wasn't scared of the water anymore and they shared the job of fetching the water."

"That's a fun story." Seth gives his approval.

"Would any of you like to tell a story that a child in Africa might tell?" I ask. "We can act it out while you tell it."

Aaron begins eagerly. "Remember," I tell him. "We've learned that if you were a child in Africa, you probably would have no TV or video games, you wouldn't have toys from a store, and most of your stories would have animals in them." I summarize some of the observations they had made about the folk tales.

Aaron nods and begins. "Once there was a boy who lived in Africa. An American person came to Africa. And he talked about TV and when the American person left they all wanted to watch it. But he didn't have TV, so he went to watch the animals and see if they did anything interesting like on TV. Then he thought *he* would be on TV, so he rode on the wolf. And there really was people from America with tapes and he was on TV!"

How could I have thought that Aaron, who gets a new Beanie Baby or video before he even has time to want it, would understand a new worldview in one day? Television, for him, is the real experience. African animals are the secondary event. I search for a comment that will not reflect the discouragement I feel. "Do you think that would be a story a real African child might tell?" I ask.

"Part of it was really about Africa," Aaron critiques his own story. "Going to the animals and watching them and having a ride on the wolf. And they *may* have heard about TV." I don't argue with his assessment.

"Does anyone else want a turn?" I ask. Kathy tries next.

"Once there were three boys and one girl and they went to the lake. They were having so much fun playing in the water that it got so late that they didn't even notice that it was very late out. All of a sudden, the first girl said, 'Look! It's getting late. I think we should go inside.' So they got out of the lake and started walking. But it was so dark, they couldn't see that they were going the wrong way. And then one of the boys said, 'I don't recognize this way.' And then the second boy said, 'I think we should still keep walking.' And the girl said, 'I agree.' And it got so dark, they had made a whole entire circle and then when it was morning, they found out they were standing right in front of their house."

"Do you think that might have been told by an African child?" I ask.

"Yeah," several children say.

"Except that African children would have had animals play the parts of humans," Rebecca adds, "like animals carrying the water on their heads."

I am elated by Kathy's story. A year older than Aaron, and an accomplished storyteller, she understood that the children in her story didn't need television or toys to have a good time. They were so happy playing in the river, they didn't notice it was getting dark. Kathy also understood intuitively that a folk tale often teaches a lesson that the culture considers important. In this story, children learn that they must not become so absorbed in their play that they don't come home on time.

What were the teaching stories of my childhood?

In my mind, I pull the large picture book of Bible stories off the shelf next to the fireplace in the living room of my childhood. The book opens almost automatically to my favorite stories of King David, and I can see the picture of young David with his slingshot aimed at a laughing Goliath. I liked the idea that even someone very small could be powerful.

The picture I loved even more came a few pages earlier. In a full page painting, David plays his harp to the mad King Saul, whose rages could only be calmed by the beautiful music. I remember rubbing my father's head to comfort him, and I wonder if King Saul had migraines too.

I think of the Deadman and Bloodman of Seth's stories, with their senseless violence. What are the teaching stories for these children? What can I do to fill the gap?

The next day at morning meeting I remind the children of their African stories. "Does anyone want to tell an African-style story to act out today?" I ask.

No one answers.

CHAPTER 19

Bottled Up

I look forward to Christmas break, with its ten precious days away from the incessant talk of sex and violence in my classroom. But when it comes, I find Seth's voice, rough and bragging, still in my head. Is there a way, I wonder, to take the energy that goes into the suicide game and channel it into something I like better? African folk tales are not the answer. But what about fairy tales? The gory, exciting adventures for the boys and for Nina. The Cinderella stories to attract the girls.

I have a collection of Cinderella stories from around the world that I know the girls will love. But what should I choose for the boys and Nina? I look for books with strong heroes who fight dragons, are brave in war, and believe in honor and justice. As I search, I notice that one major difference between these stories and the ones the boys take from television is that the fairy tales always end well, with the hero or heroine justly rewarded and the evil characters suitably punished.

Still searching for books for the boys, I pick up my old copy of *The Uses of Enchantment,* published by Bettelheim in 1975, while I was still at the Orthogenic School. In it, he talks about the underlying meaning of many fairy tales.

> Just because his life is often bewildering to him, the child needs even more to be given the chance to understand himself in this complex world with which he must learn to cope. To be able to do so, the child must be helped to make some coherent sense out of the turmoil of his

> feelings. He needs ideas on how to bring his inner house into order, and on that basis be able to create order in his life. He needs—and this hardly requires emphasis at this moment in our history—a moral education which subtly, and by implication only, conveys to him the advantages of moral behavior: not through abstract ethical concepts but through that which seems tangibly right and therefore meaningful to him. The child finds this kind of meaning through fairy tales. (page 5)

Bettelheim is right. I wouldn't mind the violence so much if it had a moral purpose. As Jason pointed out when he told me about *Amistad,* senseless violence is the most disturbing.

I continue to thumb through Bettelheim's book, looking for a story that will be meaningful to my boys. A title I don't recognize catches my eye. It's called "The Fisherman and the Jinny."

A poor fisherman has cast his net four times, each time bringing up less than the time before. On the fourth try, he brings in a copper jar, opens it, and a Jinny (genie) comes out and threatens to kill the poor fisherman. The Jinny explains that during the first hundred years that he was confined in the bottle, he told himself, "Whoso shall release me, him will I enrich forever and ever." But the full century went by, and when no one set him free, he said, "Whoso shall release me, for him I will open the hoards of the earth." After the fourth century, he said, "Whoso shall release me, for him I will fulfill three wishes." Yet no one set him free. The Jinny told the fisherman, "Thereupon I waxed wroth with exceeding wrath and said to myself, 'Whoso shall release me from this time forth, him will I slay'" (page 29).

The fisherman tricks the Jinny to get into the bottle, and he throws it safely back in the ocean.

Yet the image of the Jinny in the bottle fascinates me, and I read on, wondering what Bettelheim makes of this story.

He says, "There is no way to know whether in the original language of 'The Fisherman and the Jinny' there is a saying similar to ours about 'bottled-up' feelings. But the image of confinement in a bottle was as apt then as it is for us now" (page 30).

I picture the normal anger of my childhood bottled up like the genie. If I could have expressed it, it would have dispersed as I moved on to other things. But when I kept it inside, for fear of making my father angry and becoming the subject of his terrible silence, it grew increasingly powerful.

Maybe Dr. B. had been partly right about my father, after all. But it was my own anger, not my father's, that had threatened to choke me. Could my fear of my own anger be connected to my antipathy toward images of violence?

CHAPTER 20

Baba Yaga

If the story "The Fisherman and the Jinny" brought me this unexpected insight, how can I predict which stories will be most important to the children? I will have to read many different stories to them, and see which ones capture their imaginations.

During the rest of my vacation, I scour the library and bookstores for fairy tales and I plan a unit I call Bread and Books. Each week we will focus on a particular culture, reading folk and fairy tales from that part of the world. On Friday, we will bake bread that is typical of that culture, and the bakers will design experiments that compare bread with and without key ingredients, like yeast, salt, and sugar. In a frozen New England winter, the Friday bread baking seems to fit well with the nurturing tone of the theme.

I am both drawn toward yet nervous about the Baba Yaga stories from Russia. Baba Yaga is a witch who lives in the forest in a hut that stands on chicken feet. Lighted skulls on a fence surround her yard. She travels in a mortar, propelling herself through the sky with a pestle. Is this too scary for my class? Should I be bringing in such violent images? Yet I know both boys and girls would love the story of the innocent girl, Vasilisa, who is sent to Baba Yaga by her wicked stepmother, ostensibly to borrow a light, but really to be rid of her. Vasilisa defeats the wicked Baba Yaga with the help of her doll, given to her by her mother before she died, who speaks to her to give her advice and comfort.

I look again through *The Uses of Enchantment,* this time to find what Bettelheim says about such violent stories. In a chapter called "Fear of Fantasy," I find his answer.

> Parents who wish to deny that their child has murderous wishes and wants to tear things and even people into pieces believe that their child must be prevented from engaging in such thoughts (as if this were possible). By denying access to stories which implicitly tell the child that others have the same fantasies, he is left to feel that he is the only one who imagines such things. This makes his fantasies really scary. On the other hand, learning that others have the same or similar fantasies makes us feel that we are a part of humanity, and allays our fears that having such destructive ideas has put us beyond the common pale. (page 122)

Feeling more confident of my choices, I bring in the books I have collected—several versions of the Baba Yaga stories as well as my Cinderella stories from around the world, and an assortment of other fairy tales. I introduce Baba Yaga carefully, showing the children the last picture before I begin to read, so they can see that the girl and her small doll are successful in the end. I tell the children that if anyone feels too frightened at any point, I will arrange for that child to go across the hall to the library. No one does. The children listen to the two versions I have brought in over and over, making large posters of the story. Then Seth triumphantly brings in a new version that he found in his library, the most exciting one yet. We decide that for the school open house next week, we will turn our dramatic play area into Baba Yaga's house. Nina draws a large picture of Baba Yaga and cuts it out to sit on a chair. The table in front of her is piled high with play food. Refrigerator boxes become Baba Yaga's fence, and Alison and Seth begin to paint the skull lanterns in gold poster paint on each side.

Seth looks at Alison's section of fence, and then scowls as he looks at the one he is painting. "Alison's is better," he says quietly. "It's the gate. I didn't put a gate on mine."

"What can Seth do to feel better?" I ask the group at the art table.

"He can make one with a gate, too," Travis suggests.

"Maybe Alison can make a gate for him, too," Gregory says.

"Okay," Alison answers, looking up from her work. "All Seth has to do is tell me where he wants it."

"Sure!" Seth tells her.

I am delighted to see the energy in the class focused on the Baba Yaga project. But I am a bit worried about the open house. What will the visiting parents think? I feel a bit like Baba Yaga myself, enticing children into my scary classroom. I'm not sure I'm ready to give up my own "good girl" image.

Before the open house, I spend the afternoon making big posters describing the scientific experiments we have done on bread, with photographs of our loaves with and without yeast and salt.

But the visiting parents, like the children, know our real focus. "Oh! Baba Yaga!" a mother exclaims as she enters the room, holding the hand of a wide-eyed blond girl. The child walks cautiously between Seth and Alison's skull lanterns, and begins to explore the hut on chicken feet.

"You know the story?" I ask the mother.

"Oh yes!" she answers. That story helped me survive high school! When things got tough, I would go to the listening center in the library, put Mussorgsky's *Pictures at an Exhibition* on the turntable, and put on the earphones. I listened to the section on Baba Yaga over and over again."

"How did that help?" I ask.

"It was something about the terror and the beauty, the strength of the emotions, that connected with my whole body not just my head," she explains.

Most parents do not know the story. Many are interested, ask questions and leaf through our picture books.

Only a few look at the posters of our scientific experiment with bread.

CHAPTER 21

Forgiveness

I overhear a conversation in the hallway that I am not intended to hear. Seth, perhaps by accident, has stepped on Joel's plastic model of a World War II fighter plane.

"Stop!" Joel tells him. "That's a Spitfire! It belongs to my father, and it's his favorite model from when he was a boy!"

Seth's foot pauses on the airplane's wing a split second longer, he looks up at Joel, and then turns and walks into the classroom.

Joel's mother, helping him put his coat and lunch box in his cubby, watches silently, her lips pressed tightly together. Joel picks up the plane and looks it over carefully. "You see what I told you?" his mother says. "He's not a nice boy."

"But I like him anyway," Joel answers firmly. "He's my friend."

I know Joel's mother worries about the influence Seth is having on her sweet son. I, too, have encouraged connections with the other young boys in the class. I assign him to a lunch table with Aaron and give him Gregory for a math partner. But from the beginning, Joel has preferred his exciting and unpredictable friendship with Seth. And each morning, I watch Joel's mother watch with disapproval as he goes straight to Seth to make plans for recess.

So later, as the children are cleaning up to go outdoors, when I hear Joel's usually soft, high voice speak out strongly, I look up immediately from the child I am helping, and pay special attention to the conversation.

"I didn't say, 'Re-nade.' I said, 'Gre-nade,'" Joel is telling Seth.

"You said, 'Re-nade,'" Seth insists, his voice louder and more emphatic.

"If you keep saying that," Joel answers, "I won't be your friend."

Good, I tell myself. Stick to your guns, Joel.

"I want to talk about this," I tell them. "Sit down a minute, and I'll be right there."

The other children head outdoors. By the time I reach Seth and Joel, the argument has changed.

"You can't take it back," Seth is demanding.

"Yes, I can," Joel tells him. He looks at me, a worried frown on his forehead, his lower lip trembling. "I was just kinda mad that Seth said I said 'renade' when I said 'grenade.' So I said he's not my friend. Now I want to take it back. He *is* my friend. But he says I can't take it back. I think that means he doesn't *want* to be my friend.

I'm disappointed that Joel is revising his statement. I want him to stop being Seth's friend if Seth continues to treat him badly.

But Seth makes a counteraccusation. "You're always complaining when I'm not on your side!"

"No!" says Joel.

"Yeah! You always beg to be on my side." Seth looks at me. "He makes me feel like I don't want to be his friend anymore, 'cause he's always annoying me."

"Is it true, then," I ask, "that you don't want to be Joel's friend?"

"I do want to be Joel's friend," Seth answers. "It just *feels* like I don't wanna be his friend because he's always annoying me when he wants to be on my side."

"But don't you want to be on his side?" I ask. "I thought you were good friends."

"We are!" Seth's voice is quiet, now. The loud belligerent tone is gone. "I mean, I don't know. I can't be on Joel's side, because he *always* wants to be on my side!"

"Okay. It's true," Joel answers. "I really like you. I don't mean to annoy you." His large eyes stare openly at Seth.

"He doesn't know that he annoys me," Seth says quietly.

I remember my earlier futile attempts to censor Seth's talk, and that when I listened to him, I learned more than I expected. I'm glad I didn't try to cut him off this time. "I think sometimes you annoy him, too," I say, hoping to make the most of this moment of openness.

Joel responds directly, as always. "You annoyed me when you stepped on my fighter plane."

"No, I didn't!" Seth's voice is loud and defensive again.

Joel persists. "You looked down and you noticed you were stepping on it. I forgive you for that, Seth."

"No!" Seth continues working on his defense. "Somebody else stepped on it. I was *barely* stepping on it. I was like this close!" He demonstrates a small distance between his thumb and his forefinger. "And then you told me to stop, so I stopped."

"One piece came a little loose," Joel tells him. "Well, Seth," he continues. "I forgive you. Even if you *don't* do it, I'll forgive you for every bad thing you do."

How I wish I could forgive Seth so easily for all he denies. "Will you forgive Joel for every bad thing he does?" I ask Seth. "That would be fair."

"Yeah," he answers solemnly. "Joel!" he continues, with the excitement of an emerging idea in his voice. "I'm not sure how we're gonna work this out. You know when we were playing mosquito tag?"

"Yeah."

"Before," Seth continues, "you were 'it,' and now we're just starting all over again. You don't want to be 'it,' or do you want to?" He looks up at Joel, waiting eagerly for his answer.

I think giving Joel the choice implies he's willing to share some of the power in their relationship, at least for the moment.

"Wait!" Joel answers. "I don't want to play mosquito tag. I'm playing Lost World with Patrick."

"I want to play!" Seth demands.

"Okay, you can. You can be one of the guys that helps us crawl through the tall grass with raptors chasing after us."

Wanting to be sure my lesson is clear, I interrupt. "Did you notice that when you're mad at each other, you both say, 'I'm not going to be your friend if you do this?' But you really don't mean it."

"Yeah," Seth answers.

"But could we talk about it some more later?" Joel asks. "So we can go out and play?"

CHAPTER 22

Keeping Calm

Coming in from recess a week later, Seth grabs paper and markers and makes a superhero in a few bold black strokes. "Look at that blood gush out!" he tells Daniel as he covers the paper with red lines.

"Time for math," I remind him. He shrugs and seems to ignore me, but as I plan my next move he puts his papers away and sits down on the rug with the other children. He makes faces at Daniel, trying to get him to laugh. "Seth," I say. "You were drawing a violent picture that doesn't follow our rules for violence, and now you're having a hard time settling down. Do you see the connection?"

"I do," Nina agrees.

"Pow!" Seth answers. "The reason we like violent games is 'cause they're fun!"

"What games that you play help you feel more settled when you come in?" I ask.

"When I play soccer," Nina answers, "I always talk about it a lot. I don't listen when we come in, 'cause we talk about who wins or who scores the most."

"So it's the competition you're talking about, not the game itself?" I ask.

"Yeah," she agrees.

"We were playing store," Kathy explains, "and it was like by accident someone gave away a pretty pinecone that another person was going to sell. And the person who was going to sell it got mad. Then, when you come in, it's all unsettled, 'cause they got all upset about it."

"So not following the rules of the game makes it hard to settle down?" I ask.

Kathy nods and continues. "I also think that when you're playing store with somebody, when you come in if you say, 'I sold the most stuff!' that's unsettled."

"That's like Nina's soccer score," I point out.

"You know how all these things are at recess?" Alison points out. "Well, I think recess is what makes us all wild."

I am reminded of the elementary schools that are cutting out recess as a waste of time and a distraction from work. But I refuse to agree with that, although I see Alison's point. It's easy for her to sit still, and for her, work is fun, like a game of school, where she can pretend to be the good student she is in real life.

"Competition and not following the rules make you unsettled," I say. "What makes you feel calm?"

"Not playing?" Alison asks. "Sitting down?"

"That would make you more wild!" Gregory exclaims. "Then you hold in all your energy! And then you blast it out of there!" After a few rainy days in a row, I have seen Gregory trying hard not to blast.

"What makes you calm is when you run around as fast as you can," Alison changes her opinion after listening to Gregory. "When you're all out of energy, you listen better at meeting."

"Before I watch *Rugrats,*" Kayla says, "I have to run around the house four times to get tired." I keep forgetting how hard it is for children to sit still.

"Let's watch for more kinds of play that make you feel calm," I suggest.

The next day, I watch the children come in from recess, sit down quietly, and appear ready to work. I'm tempted to begin my math lesson quickly, while I have everyone's attention, but I decide to risk losing the calm moment to find out what they did at recess.

"It was fun," Seth tells me. "We played Goosebumps."

This was not the answer I wanted to hear. *Goosebumps* is a hor-ror series for children.

"What made you so calm this time?" I ask.

"Well," Seth explains, "there was two people on each side. And we had no problems and no fights."

"So fairness made it go well?" I ask.

"And we didn't cheat." Seth adds, "by not falling down when someone shoots you."

"I think what makes play calmer is not getting so hyped up and doing one hundred things at once," Kathy says. "Instead, I made one basket out of sticks for our store."

"So, Kathy," I tell her, "if you feel yourself getting hyper, maybe you can remind yourself to slow down. Seth, what can you do?"

"Play Goosebumps," he answers.

"Not playing winning games is what I do," Joel adds.

"When I'm hyper," Gregory says, "I rest."

"Whenever I want to do something and I see I can't do it," Nina says, "I just stop what I'm doing and take some deep breaths, and start over."

The children tell me it's not the violent content of the games that makes them upset. If their game is fair, if they play by the rules, and if it doesn't get too competitive, they feel settled whether or not the content of their fantasy is violent. Is my theory about violence in play all wrong? Maybe I need to stop what I'm doing, take some deep breaths, and start over.

CHAPTER 23

Half Bulldog, Half Chihuahua

"Was there anything at recess that made you so unsettled?" I ask one day when the children seem especially restless.

"I was playing a game outside," Joel begins, "and Daniel was the big brother and he said I was a teenager and I was smoking and I would have to get out of the house and live on the streets. I didn't like it."

"That's how the game goes!" Daniel explains.

"No." I jump in quickly. "It's not. That's like saying 'You can't play.'" Although I like the children to make their own rules, I do not allow them to exclude each other.

"But it's the only person left!" Daniel insists. "Seth's the brother, Kayla's the sister, and Alison is the mother."

"I think it's not nice to make someone do something like make somebody move out on to the street," Kathy says, "and say that's the only part left in the game. He can be a person in the family, like there could be two uncles or two brothers."

"What do you think a fair rule would be about this?" I ask.

"That you can be whatever you want," Alison answers.

"Then I'm not playing," Daniel announces. "'Cause I want to go by the *rules* of this game, and that's not the rule! And I already have too much brothers and sisters and cousins and uncles."

"It sounds like everyone got a part they wanted except Joel," I point out.

"Because he joined in last!" Daniel explains. "It was the only part left!"

I hold firm. "You can't play the kind of game where someone gets left out." I insist.

"I think he can choose what he wants to be," Travis agrees with me. "Last year, I wanted to join a game and there was no good parts left, 'cause I wanted to be a good guy and there was only bad guys left. The kids who were playing made a new part for me." Travis is the youngest child in the class. He is the pet and mascot of the oldest boys in the school, and a welcome playmate of children his own age. I know a good part will always be invented for him.

Gregory agrees with Travis. "I think Joel could be anything but the parts that are already in it," he says.

"Like a dog," Nina adds.

"Yeah!" Daniel agrees. "That's what I was gonna say!"

"How about a Chihuahua?" Gregory asks.

"A bulldog!" Nina says.

"How about half bulldog, half Chihuahua?" Seth suggests.

"Okay," Joel agrees.

"I'm the mom," Alison says. "I didn't realize that you didn't want to be homeless, Joel."

"I told everyone," Joel answers.

"Next time, tell me," Alison says.

"Okay," Joel tells her happily. "I will."

CHAPTER 24

Exorcising the Exorcist

Why do the children find violent images so appealing? I look for Jason in the morning, hoping he can help me understand. "Would you be willing to come and talk with me again?" I ask.

Later that afternoon, he meets me when my children are at recess. He takes a large package of Smarties candy from the pocket of his cargo pants and sits down.

"When I see violence on television," I say, "I identify with the person being killed and I feel sick. You see both sides of many situations in real life, so how is it that the violent movies don't bother you?"

"It's sort of like, you must get trained," he says, putting a handful of candies in his mouth. "It's like in the military, when they saw that not very many people were shooting their guns, they started training them to think that it was okay to shoot, you know, and like when you play a violent game, you play it enough, you almost start getting trained to kill and not thinking about who you're killing. I think that's what happens. As a kid sees enough violent stuff, he doesn't think about the pain that the other person would go through. He thinks about the good things, like the bad guy's dead.

"Partly it's like if you think enough about it, it starts not being scary anymore. Like I saw this movie at my friend's house and I thought it was really very scary. And I went over to his house again and we saw it again, and it wasn't that scary that time, but it was still pretty scary and we watched it again and again and little by little it started getting less scary until it wasn't scary at all."

I wonder if it could be that what scares you is bad and can be killed with impunity.

"It's like the same thing with fear," he continues. "I remember when I was a little kid. I used to be afraid to put my head out of the blanket at night. And then eventually, over the years, I got less and less afraid and I would sort of peek out sometimes. And then when I got to be like nine years old I would go to sleep with my head out as long as I kept my eyes shut. And when I got to be ten, I could lie in bed with my eyes open. And then I went over to my friend's house and we saw this really scary movie and it sort of brought the whole thing back, it sort of like hit the reset button. I get these images in my head at night, like I'd stick my head out and I'd imagine like a disgusting image like popping up from like over the side of my bed and it's really scary. Something from *The Exorcist*. That's what the movie was." Jason puts another large handful of Smarties into his mouth and chews while he continues.

"And when my friend told me about a movie where someone has the power to make people stab themselves with pitchforks, well, before I had seen *The Exorcist,* that wouldn't have been really scary to me. But it adds on, it builds up. I think it's the same thing with violence. Once you get used to it, it's really hard to reset the button unless you experience something really violent."

While Jason speaks, I have an image of myself at age six at the amusement park at Revere Beach. I was afraid of all the rides. I wouldn't consider trying the roller coasters. I wouldn't even go on the bumper cars. I watched my mother and my brother happily bumping into each other, heard the squeals of delight, but even with the tantalizing idea of getting behind the wheel, I couldn't bring myself to try it out. Anything that made me afraid was to be avoided.

Jason's use of movies to master his fears works only when the movie is scary enough to satisfy his sense of mastery without being so frightening that it "resets the button" and brings on a new set of anxieties. If he can predict the movie well enough, avoiding images that are too disturbing, he can tame his childhood fears.

If Seth saw *The Exorcist* with only his six years of life experience to help him sort out real from pretend, he would have more difficulty knowing which of the awful events in the movie were realistically possible and which ones could never happen. He might have to rely on magical thinking to protect himself from the fears the movie raised, pretending he had powers or hidden strengths. He might use the influence he has over his friends to make him feel more powerful and less vulnerable. Or he might act out his fantasies in pretend play, making himself feel stronger by being the master who can make Gregory explode and disintegrate in the suicide game.

"Is there anything that's helped you get over that fear of *The Exorcist*?" I ask Jason.

"Well, sometimes what I do to myself is I say, 'Okay, if this person came after you, what would you do?' My brother told me about this scary movie called *The Shining,* and there's this guy and he's trying to kill someone so he locks himself in the bathroom and the guy's trying to chop down the door with an ax. And then he chops a crack in the door. I saw the previews and it shows the part where he sticks his head through the crack and so I'm trying to figure out a way to get that out of my mind. And I think of him as Jack Nicholson because he didn't have that much stage makeup on. If he stuck his head through my bathroom door, I would ask him for his autograph. And that sort of helps."

"I had a really weird dream last night," Jason continues, "I think inspired by that idea, that I was in the room with this guy and he hung himself on a guitar string from one of my lights up on the ceiling. And he was talking and he told me his name was Jack Nicholson and he wanted my autograph! That sort of helped me; to think of it in a silly way."

"If you could rewind your life and go right back to before you saw *The Exorcist*," I ask him, "would you see it?"

"If I knew what it would do to me? No. I would have said, 'I don't want to watch this.' But once you start watching it, you want to watch it more, 'cause if it's an exciting movie, you want to know what happens in the end. And some parts, I just covered my eyes, 'cause I wanted to know what happens, but I didn't want to see some of it.

"What I like is if it's scary while you watch it, but it doesn't stay in your mind. I saw this movie about people that find this huge spacecraft and there's a golden sphere and if you go inside it your thoughts become real. And so I just wondered if your mind makes up what you're afraid of, and that made me think about like if I was really afraid about a guy who comes in the middle of the night, I could make him go away if I stop thinking about him. And that really helped me, 'cause I think it's true."

"What is it about a movie that makes it too scary?" I ask.

"*The Exorcist* was the first movie I saw that made it too scary," he answers. "It's the images of the girl's face and her voice that were really disturbing." He comforts himself with a large handful of Smarties.

"She had long brown hair and her face was completely drained and she has all these cuts and scars from times when she tried to like move stuff with her eyes and I don't know, and then her nose is like pulled back and she has a cord in her nose. And there's this part where the mother goes in her room and the girl was stabbing herself with a knife and the mother starts to grab the knife and the girl looks at the mother really carefully and the mother goes like flying down and then this huge chair blocks the door so no one else can come in the room and then this like bookshelf falls down on her mom's legs so her mom can't get up and then the girl's head turns around like a hundred and eighty degrees and is looking at the mother like smiling. Those images were really scary.

"In *The X Files*," he explains, "it's like someone is selling all of us. It was scary, but afterwards I can sort of say, 'No, that just couldn't happen.' But it's harder when people's bodies go out of control. There's also a difference between violence and fear. Because if there's a lot of shooting and a lot of people die, I don't think that's such a good thing but I don't really feel very affected by it later. But if it's that someone can't control themselves, that's more scary."

I wonder if it's harder to separate the bad, kill it off and be rid of it if the bad part is inside.

I think about my avoidance of bumper cars. What is my equivalent of Jason's watching a movie over and over, becoming a little less afraid each time? Suddenly I know. By putting my fear on paper, stretching it out and looking at it without blinking, I gain mastery so that I, too, can keep my eyes open and my head out of the covers.

CHAPTER 25

Tortured

Sarah, my sixteen-year-old, asks me to take her to see the movie *Elizabeth*.

I look at the ad in the paper. "You know how I feel about R-rated movies," I tell her. "Does it have sex or violence?"

"Both, probably," she admits cheerfully. "But it's not *really* violent," she reassures me. "It's historical fiction."

I put her off. "I don't see movies that are rated R unless I know what the violence is going to be," I explain to her. "After they're over, I can't get the violent scenes out of my head."

For the next two months, she keeps me informed of where *Elizabeth* is being shown and the awards it has won. I watch it move farther away, relieved but guilty.

The children in my class would not flinch at a few bloody war scenes. Why am I so afraid? I can't stand to see scenes of violence. I don't even have a television.

Am I afraid, like Jason, of monsters under the bed? A killer outside the shower might give me nightmares, but surely not a queen who lived 450 years ago.

Am I afraid of death? I cried through Beth's slow demise from tuberculosis in *Little Women,* but I wouldn't miss it.

Is it the blood and guts? The battlefield of Atlanta was disturbing, but I took Sarah to see *Gone with the Wind* on the big screen.

Now my curiosity is engaged. I begin to wonder if I did go to

see *Elizabeth,* if I could watch my own reactions and try to understand more precisely what it is that I wish so intensely to avoid. Is
there a specific type of scene I can't stand to see? Could I catch myself taking pleasure in watching a violent act?

I find myself checking the paper to see if it's still around, then
making arrangements for us to go.

At the theater, I arm myself with coffee and popcorn, while
Sarah prefers Coke and sour gummy bears.

As the movie opens, three Protestant heretics are getting their
heads shaved by a man with an ax, then tied to stakes and set on
fire. Sarah and I chew fiercely as a crowd of Catholic adults and
children enjoy the scene, the fire burning higher around the
screaming captives. As I fight a strong desire to turn away, I realize
that the flames are leaving no marks on their bodies or on the
background scene. The picture of fire has been superimposed over
the screaming actors. I watch, fascinated, like Jason seeing a movie
over and over until he is no longer afraid.

I find myself intrigued with the story of the young Elizabeth,
just a little older than Sarah, who is childishly eager to become
queen. Initially delighted by her power, she gradually becomes
aware of the precariousness of her position as she discovers that
most of her friends, including her lover, have plotted against her.
She becomes increasingly independent, crafty and coldhearted.

A messenger of the pope, captured on his way to the traitors, is
hanged from the ceiling by his hands and feet, his arms gradually
pulled from his sockets. My stomach knots and my own shoulder
aches as I tighten against the scene. This time, I find nothing to en-
gage my intellectual curiosity, and although I force myself not to
turn away, I do not feel the exhilaration that comes with mastering my fear that might make my discomfort seem worthwhile.
Unlike Jason, simply watching is not enough to make me feel
better.

As the traitors are about to be beheaded, the executioner's ax
is raised, and the scene fades to the clouds. I am reminded of the
guillotine scene in *A Tale of Two Cities.* There too, as Ronald Col-
man is about to lose his head, the camera switches to the clouds
above, the music swells, and we hear the guillotine fall on the

brave Sydney Carton. *Elizabeth,* however, is a movie of the nineties, and in the next moment we see the three heads impaled on the castle gateposts. I prefer the old style.

Now I know what repels me most. It's the cruelty of people taking pleasure in treating one another viciously. Both the characters in the story and the people in the movie audience enjoy watching human beings tortured. I find being in that position intolerable.

Unexpectedly, I am transported back forty years to a holiday dinner at my grandparents' house. After I have finished my grandmother's chicken soup made especially for me, and succumbed to her admonitions to have "just one more *kichlach,*" my favorite sugar-dipped cookie, I am sitting on the plastic-covered chair in the pastel blue living room, when my grandfather notices me from across the room. "Tema! Tema!" He calls me by my middle name, patting the empty seat on the couch next to him. Ambivalently, I walk over and sit down by him. "Tema!" he says again, his voice tremulous, as he pats my cheek, his eyes wet. Named after his sister who died in a concentration camp, I know she lives in me in some way I cannot fully understand. I both look forward to and dread this ritual, liking the attention but afraid of the part of me that was exterminated by the Nazis.

Now, identifying so intensely with the one being tortured, I cannot stand to get enjoyment from watching a scene like the burning of the heretics. It is as though I am one of them, and the audience is enthralled, watching me die, too. Is that why I am afraid to look? Is that why I don't even have television, to make sure I don't enjoy watching someone else's suffering?

I leave the movie feeling pleased with my new insight, and glad I had not let my fear of violence make me avoid this astonishing performance. "I wonder if there's a good biography of Elizabeth," I tell Sarah on the way home. "I'd like to know more about her. And I wouldn't mind seeing the movie again, just to watch how she makes the transition from the naive adolescent into the brilliant queen. But I wouldn't mind seeing it on video, so we could skip over that first torture scene."

"Me, too," Sarah admits, and smiles at me.

CHAPTER 26

Mama's Little Baby

The children clamor around me at their cubbies, all talking at once. "Seth beat up on Joel," Aaron's clear young voice carries through the din.

I am not surprised that Joel and Seth are having trouble again, but I am surprised to hear about a fight. Although this group loves violence in fantasy, they are rarely physically hurtful in real life. I tell the children to get started on their math project while I talk with Patrick and Seth, who are slowly hanging up their jackets.

"What happened at recess?" I ask them.

Seth avoids my eyes, looking instead at his new Batman sneakers that light up at every step. He taps his heel on the floor, and we watch the light go on and off.

"Well," he begins. "I started fighting and Joel started grabbing my head and twisting it to get me down on the wood chips."

I appreciate Seth's honesty in admitting he started the fight, but I am skeptical that Joel, a year younger and much smaller than Seth, would grab his head to pull him down.

"What happened before that?" I ask.

"Joel called us 'Mama's little baby,'" Seth answers. And then me and Patrick jumped on Joel, right, Patrick?"

" 'Cause we don't like it," Patrick confirms. "We didn't tell the teacher"—he pauses, anticipating my next question—" 'cause we forgot with our minds."

I notice Aaron hanging around the doorway to the cubby

room, waiting to see if someone is going to get in trouble. "Would you ask Joel to come here?" I ask him.

Joel arrives quickly.

"Were you calling Seth, 'Mama's little baby'?" I ask him.

"No." Joel answers without hesitating. "They were saying it to me." His clear hazel eyes look directly into mine, and I believe him. "Seth and Patrick did it." He looks at Seth.

"He was on the monkey bars, and I started yelling, 'Mama's little baby.'" Seth has a new version, apparently disregarding his earlier explanation. "Joel," he continues, "remember when I started wrestling?"

"No," Joel answers. "That was Patrick."

"Oh, I didn't know," Seth explains. "Me and Patrick started the game yesterday. We were calling Joel 'Mama's little baby' and chasing him, and he didn't seem to mind. And then today, me and Patrick started calling him that and he got mad. And me and Patrick ran away. Then Joel came back and Daniel came over and started calling us 'Mama's little baby.'" I thought Joel was doing it, so I got mad at him when he wasn't really doing it."

Still confused, I decide to try a shortcut. "Would you all like to agree to stop calling one another 'Mama's little baby?' at the same time?"

"We already stopped," Seth explains. "We use guns now, instead of 'Mama's little baby.'" He points his finger and cocks his thumb in the traditional shooting position.

"Is that working better?" I ask, surprised.

"Yeah!" All three agree.

I am reminded that Barney Brawer, in a seminar I took at Tufts called Studying Boys in the Early Childhood Classroom, described the way some boys throw insults at each other. In his theory of "the worthy opponent," he described boys who look for partners in play who can throw insults back and forth the way tennis players look for opponents who can hit the ball back to them with equal skill. At five and six, young boys are better at throwing insults than they are at catching them.

"Maybe name-calling is sometimes a game like pretend shooting," I tell the three boys in front of me, "but some people like it and some don't."

"My friend Jess and me play that game," Seth agrees. "She likes it."

"He can call me 'numskull,' " Joel suggests.

"That means you don't have any brains," Patrick explains.

"No," Joel disagrees. "It means your brain has tentacles."

Why is 'numskull' acceptable, when 'Mama's little baby' is worth fighting over? Seth and Patrick are working hard to outgrow being Mama's babies themselves. Seth's father tells me he is concerned that he still sucks his thumb at night. Only last year, at five, these boys kissed their mothers good-bye in the mornings in the cubby room, while now they proudly walk into the building themselves, backpacks slung over their shoulders. If they can put all their babyish feelings onto Joel, who is younger and sweeter than they are, perhaps by excluding him they can try to get rid of their own feelings of dependence. Does that exclusion justify, in their minds, being violent toward him, as they attempt to stamp out all the babyishness around them?

Joel, happy to be shot or called 'numskull,' is unwilling to be called 'Mama's little baby,' even if it means he is excluded from their play. If he would throw an insult back at them, he might be accepted. Do I have to teach him to be tough?

When I see Nate a few mornings later, I decide to ask his advice. "Did you ever want to be friends with someone who was mean to you?" I ask him.

"Well, yeah," he answers slowly, as though reluctant to begin. He sits on the art table, watching me set up tools for woodworking. "Tony was my friend, except for when he was with Caleb. I remember one time when Caleb called me a girl. Then he punched me for no reason. I could have got him sent home from school for that, but I did not tell. People say, 'If you tell, I won't be your friend.' But I guess they're not a good friend if they punch you."

"Mama's little baby" or "girl," the parallel is clear. Being seen as weak justifies being attacked by those who want to be strong.

"Why would a kid go on trying to be friends with that person?" I ask Nate.

"I never really cared for Caleb," he answers. "But he was always hanging out with Tony, and I liked Tony. I was kind of soft," he adds. "They were tougher kids. I thought they would keep pickin' on me, if I told."

"Is there anything an adult could do to help in that situation?" I ask.

"Eventually, we just got separated in different classes, and I made new friends," Nate answers. "But what really helps is to ask the kid, 'Do you like him? Do you think he's a good friend?' If he says, 'Well, he picks on me,' ask him, 'Then why do you like him? He's not a good friend if he picks on you. Maybe it's time to make a new friend.' That's what my mom told me."

I don't think Joel would accept that advice from me any more than Nate was able to use it when his mother gave it to him. I don't expect Seth's changed attitude toward Joel is more than temporary. I decide to look for help.

CHAPTER 27

Puppy Power

On the weekend, I go up the long hill to my friend Jorie's house to talk about my boys. "I still don't understand why they hit Joel and pushed him down," I tell her. "I've called their parents, asking them to talk with their boys about the incident, and I know that they will all be on their best behavior when they come back to school on Monday, but I'm still so angry at them, I don't want to face them."

Jorie is a teacher and a naturalist, and she has invited me to see her six-week-old puppies. She is planting the last row of peas in her garden as we talk.

"The biggest puppy is Rex," she tells me, pointing to a soft pup that looks like a plush black-and-white teddy bear, with two black circles around his eyes and a white stripe down his nose. We watch Rex pull the end of a bone out of the mouth of a slightly smaller puppy and run away with it.

"The smaller pup is Toby," Jorie says. I watch to see if Toby will try to get the stolen bone back, but he just looks around, sees a stick on the ground, and picks it up in his mouth. Rex drops the bone and starts to pull on the end of Toby's stick. Toby makes an attempt to hold on to it, but Rex knocks him over with a push of his paw and pulls the stick away from him. Toby puts his head down, rolls over on his back with his tail wagging, and then gets up and runs off, nosing an old plastic coffee cup as if to say "I didn't care about that old stick, anyway."

"Toby has the least interest in overwhelming the other pups," Jorie says. "He'll guard his food with a growl, but will just give in to Rex, who is larger and has more energy. Rex continually works to keep command over any situation."

"He reminds me of Seth!" I tell her about the way Seth tried to gain power, first by knowing more about violent movies than the other boys, then by planning an exciting party and leaving Joel out, and finally by trying to get Joel to give him his Popsicle stick weapons. "Like Rex, he's never satisfied. He always wants what someone else has."

We watch the puppies try to pin each other down in mock battles. "In a pack of social carnivores," Jorie explains, "it makes sense to have a hierarchy in place. If their survival depends on hunting, the stronger, more energetic, and smarter dogs will bring back the most food and get the biggest shares. You might say that their superior hunting means there will be more food for the other members of the pack, and especially for the young. At the same time, the less powerful dog can stay home and protect the puppies. The smaller dog who minds the pups is as important to the pack as the stronger ones who bring back the food."

Sparky, the large, black-and-white father of the pups, lies down on the grass in the sun. A moment later, Toby comes over, nuzzles Sparky's mouth, and soon the two are playing. First Toby grabs Sparky's upper jaw. Then Sparky gently holds Toby's muzzle between his teeth. They wrestle for a few minutes, then Toby holds still and Sparky lets go.

"They're so gentle with each other," I observe, "even when they have their teeth inside each other's mouths."

"When Toby holds still or yelps," Jorie explains, "it's a signal that he gives up, so Sparky lets go. The pups are learning to play better—they hardly ever hurt each other. Having sorted out the hierarchy early on, with constant play and constant stealing, they know their place in the power structure."

"What about Toby?" I ask. "Would the others leave him out and hurt him on purpose, like Seth and Joel?"

"If Toby is wrestling with Rex, and Belle, the leading female, joins, Toby will be excluded by the dominant pair. Then when they're done and they want to go exploring, he can join them. They won't hurt Toby, though, when he tries to get in on the play. They would only hurt an outsider, an intruder coming into their territory."

"Maybe when the stronger boys call a weaker boy 'mama's little baby' or 'girl,' they make him an outsider," I wonder out loud. "And Joel is new to the class this year."

"When there is an intruder," Jorie says, "the dogs unleash their aggression. They'll fight until the intruder is chased away."

"That sounds like what happened when Seth and Daniel beat up on Joel," I say. "They couldn't explain why they did it. I wonder if there's a way I can help the others see Joel as a member of the group, rather than an outsider."

As we head up to the house for a cup of tea, we see a muddy brown-and-white puppy coming from behind the compost, an old cornstalk held high in her mouth. "There's Belle," Jorie says. The other puppies run to her. Rex takes the cornstalk away from her and runs off with it, while Toby licks her mouth and bites her muzzle, his tail waving eagerly.

We sit down in the kitchen, and as we begin to drink our tea, Belle is at the glass door, looking up at Jorie and wagging her tail excitedly. "Look at how Belle is trying to get my attention. The boys must have done something wrong," Jorie tells me. "Let's go see what it is." We open the door and look around the corner of the house. Toby and Rex have knocked over the garbage can and are pawing through the contents. "Belle is the quickest to learn the rules and she becomes upset when they're broken. She wants me to come take care of it," Jorie explains. "She loves to explore. She's the first one to run off in the woods after a new smell or sound. She's also everyone's favorite playmate, because she doesn't try to overwhelm the pup she's playing with. Her play never ends in a fight."

"That's like Nina," I say. "So many children follow her and want to play with her. They give her power, and she uses it to look after the whole group. One day, she was a soccer captain, and when she began to pick her team, she picked Aaron, who is young and is usually picked last. I watched the disbelief cross his face. 'Yes!' he shouted, throwing his arms up in the air when she motioned for him to stand next to her. She chose a couple of strong players, and then picked Travis, who adores her but is not a popular choice. Afterward, I asked her how she picked her team. 'Aaron and Travis never get picked first,' she said. 'I thought it would be fun. And we still tied,' she added proudly."

"She must be really confident of her power," Jorie says, "to be able to do that."

"She doesn't struggle for it, the way Seth does," I tell her. "I wondered, after she ran away last fall, if I had encouraged her to think she doesn't have to follow the rules. But as I listen to you, I have a different idea. My job is to help her learn to use her strength wisely, for the good of the group, without becoming carried away by her own wish for adventure."

"Will it affect your teaching, imagining your class as a pack of dogs?" Jorie asks.

"It makes me feel less angry at Seth and Patrick," I tell her.

"How?" she wonders.

I think a moment, trying to clarify the change for myself as well as for her. "When we started talking, I was upset that after all the discussions I've had with the children about exclusion, they would still treat each other so badly. I thought, 'They should know better!' and I even wondered if everything we had done this year was worthless.

"I know the children's lives are more complex than those of your puppies. Still, if I imagine that in some ways Seth's wish to test his power is similar to Rex's need to try to dominate the other puppies, it's easier for me to remember that my job is to continue to teach him to listen to the other children's point of view. I can appeal to his sense of fairness to help him have more compassion, but I can't expect the issue to disappear.

"Do you know the story of the empty boat by the Chinese poet Chuang Tzu?" I ask. Jorie shakes her head. "As Stephen Levine tells it in *Who Dies,* a man is crossing a river in his boat when he sees another boat coming toward him. It looks as though the boat will collide with him. If he sees someone in that other boat, he yells, waves his arms, shakes his oar at him, and calls him names. When the other boat hits his, he's angry.

"But Chuang Tzu says that if that man realizes that no one is in that other boat, he doesn't feel the anger, he doesn't take it personally. And when that empty boat moves toward him, he is as careful to protect that other boat as his own. There's no anger. There's just this empty boat moving toward his and when he's pushed it aside, he goes on, without resentment.

"The work is the same, whether the boat is empty or full," I say. "I'll try to remember that Seth isn't challenging my authority to be mean or malicious, he's just testing his power to see how strong he is, just as I'm like Belle, trying to keep my whole pack safe and happy."

CHAPTER 28

The Baby Business

"Seth said a bad word," Aaron complains to me one day at lunch-time. I look at him, standing at my eye level as I sit on a small chair eating my salad. He smiles nervously and pushes his long blond hair out of his eyes. "It's the S-word," he says, his big eyes hopeful that I'll get it now. The S-word, I wonder? I remember the day he said the F-word was "frow up." What begins with *s*? "You know," as he sees my puzzled face. "S-e-x," he spells out. Aaron is a good speller.

I walk over to the lunch table where Seth and Daniel sit with Alison and Kayla. "He said he wants to cut off parts of our Barbies," the girls tell me, outraged. I don't ask what parts. Seth has a smile on his face that reminds me of an ad I saw during a re-cent showing of *The Wizard of Oz*. "Diamonds are beautiful," the middle-aged man said with a sly smile. "Especially when that's all she's got on!" I was shocked that this was shown during *Oz*. What do children think when they hear that? I remember that the other day I'd heard Seth talking to Daniel. "Poison Ivy would look bet-ter in boots, not high heels," he said in his teenage voice. "That girl was sexy!"

Sexy superheroes and cutting up the Barbies make me wonder about the connection, in some of the PG- or R-rated movies the children are seeing, between sex and violence. Can I help discon-nect the two, and make "s-e-x" a word we can discuss?

I see my chance when I have an opportunity to mate Snowflake, our pet rabbit, with Smudge, a male in another class. Two weeks later, Gregory notices the white balls of fur that she has pulled out to begin lining her nest. He shows Travis. "Are those eggs?" Travis asks. The fluffy balls do look about the size and color of small eggs.

"I don't think so," Nina says. "One looks roundish and one looks straightish, and I don't think eggs look straight like that."

"I think the roundish shape could be an egg, and the fur one next to it could be like, the fur," Kathy says.

"Maybe tomorrow we could let Snowflake out of her cage and we can feel for whether it's fur or eggs," Travis suggests.

"I *know* bunnies are born alive," Daniel tells him.

"Chickens have eggs and other birds have eggs," Gregory elaborates on Daniel's idea. "Bunnies and other birth animals don't have eggs. They're not mammals."

He has the connection right, even if the name is wrong.

"That's true," Joel agrees. I'm not surprised that he would know. He's done a lot of reading about animals. But then he startles me with his reasoning. " 'Cause sometimes eggs are a little bigger than this."

"Remember the book you read to us about the bunnies?" Kathy says to me. "The mother pulled out her fur to make her nest. I think Snowflake's doing that!"

"I agree with Kathy, sort of," Travis says. Although he originally asked if they were rabbit eggs, he has been persuaded by the strength of the arguments, and especially by the memory of the photograph Kathy called up.

Alison looks at me. "Do you know if it's eggs?" she asks.

"What you figured out was exactly right," I tell her. "Two weeks ago, Snowflake spent the weekend with Smudge, a male rabbit. Now she's pulling out her fur to line her nest. Maybe she's going to have babies. Bunnies are mammals, they have their babies alive, they don't lay eggs."

"Oh! Oh!" They gasp in delight. "Will we get to see them?"

"If she has babies, we'll keep them for two months. Then they'll be old enough to give to other classes for pets."

"Will we be able to hold them?" Seth asks. Originally the lascivious smiler, he is now as eager as any of them. "I was at a farm once, and I got to hold a baby lamb."

"Not right away," I tell them. "But when they're a little bigger. I know you'll all be gentle with them." In fact, I've never had a class that consistently treated Snowflake so well. In the beginning of the year, they wanted her to be a part of their games. They would pretend she was a robber as she hopped into the dramatic play space. Their loud "bang, bang," and sudden movements startled her, and she spent the rest of the morning behind the bookshelf, chewing noisily on the collection of papers that had fallen there out of reach. The children quickly learned that if they touched her gently and spoke quietly, she would spend most of the morning hopping from one to another, asking to be petted. I could tell by her calm behavior that no one ever gave her a sly squeeze or a quick pull on her fur.

"I want you to be especially careful with her now," I tell them. "If she does have babies growing inside her, she might be a little more sensitive to being poked or treated roughly."

"What if food splashes on the babies?" Travis asks. "While they're in her stomach?"

"Actually," I tell him, "they don't grow in her stomach. They have a special, protected place to grow."

"They don't grow *inside* the stomach," Travis elaborates. They *grow* when they come *out*."

"What's the box for?" Alison asks, pointing to the nesting box I'd put in a few days before.

"That's a safe place for the babies to grow," I tell her.

"That's where the bloody poops go," Seth says, laughing. I scold him for being silly, but later I wonder what he meant. Had he seen a birth and worried about the blood? But when I ask him, he denies having said it. Either he's too embarrassed to tell me what worried him, or he was just being silly.

"Do the babies grow in her intestines?" Joel asks. He watches animal shows on television and has picked up many words he doesn't quite understand.

"It's called the womb," I tell him. "It's near the stomach, but separate from it."

"Wait, I thought it was the kidneys?" he asks again. The children laugh. Maybe they hear the word "kid" and think he's made it up.

"The kidney is another inside part of the body that is hard to understand," I tell him.

"If she does have babies," Alison says, "could we feed them a little carrot?"

"Yes," I say.

"But why is it protected from the stomach?" Joel pursues his understanding of the connections inside the body.

"So the food won't hit it in the face," Travis explains to him. I'm glad to see he took in my earlier statement.

"What part does the baby come out?" Alison asks.

"The mouth," Travis answers quickly, continuing with the stomach theory that he had just refuted.

"Just like there's a special place in Snowflake's body for the babies to grow, there's a special place for them to come out, called the vagina," I explain. Children laugh. They've heard this is a word you're not supposed to say.

"I'm not trying to make people laugh," Travis says.

"I know you're not," I tell him. "I'm glad you asked. Some people are laughing because it makes them a little uncomfortable, but it's not funny."

"It's not funny," Aaron agrees, "but it feels as though we can't hold it in." I remember that he was the one who had to spell 'sex.'

"Everybody comes from a mom," Seth tells him.

"Not me!" Joel points out. "I was adopted!"

"You did have a birth mom, though," I remind him. He nods, seriously.

"How do animals get milk from their mothers?" Alison continues to ask important questions. But I cut her off. "We'll talk about that next time," I say. I'm pleased with how well the discussion has gone, but don't want to push it too far. Maybe I'm picking up subliminal restlessness from the children, maybe I've had all I can take at one sitting. I know we'll come back to nursing babies another day.

"Now that we're studying animal babies," I say, changing the subject, "I'll bring in some baby ducklings and some monarch caterpillars, too."

"Baby ducklings! Oh!" they exclaim.

"We'll be in the baby business!" Alison announces.

CHAPTER 29

The Finger

"He gave me the finger!" Seth shouts, running toward me at recess. The contrast between his smiling face and Joel's frightened look as he runs behind him is as stark as the difference between Seth's tall, strong body and Joel's small, frail one.

"He covered his hand," Joel explains in self-defense, "and he put up one finger, and I thought it was the middle one, so I did it back to him. But then he showed me his hand, and it was the other finger."

"*He* gave *me* the finger," Seth gloats. "I didn't do it." He demonstrates his trick, which does look pretty convincing.

"I think tricking Joel to get him in trouble is at least as hurtful as his giving you the finger," I tell Seth sternly. "We'll talk about this when we go inside." Seth smiles briefly, acknowledging he's been caught, while Joel looks relieved. They run back to the pine grove, where the most active fantasy play takes place, farthest from the teachers' watchful eyes.

I check my watch. If I don't have to settle any more fights, I have exactly five minutes to figure out how to discuss this finger episode with the whole class. Why didn't I give them both a time-out and forget about it?

When everyone is settled indoors on the rug, I describe the incident.

"Why can't you swear, anyway?" Seth demands in a belligerent tone.

"They're bad words," Gregory tells him.

"The words people use for swearing are called bad words," I explain, "but often they are good words used in a hurtful way. If you say, 'I love God,' then 'God' is not a swear word. But if you use it to be rude, then it's considered a swear."

"Like, 'Oh my God!'" Nina explains.

"What?" Gregory says, surprised, "My dad says that!"

"If I made an invention," Daniel says, "my mom would say, 'Oh my God! You actually made that?'"

"My dad's a minister," Alison says. "He gets mad if I say that."

"It depends on how you say it," I explain. "If Nina gave me the pencil she's holding, and I said, 'Thanks!' that's polite. But if I said it in an angry way"—I put my hands on my hips and sneer—"'*Tha-anks!*' that would be rude."

"You're saying it in a meaner tone of voice," Kathy points out.

"Since families are different," I explain, "in school we don't use language that some people consider rude. Most of those words have to do with things that are most special to people like religion or like the parts of the body that are considered private, about sex."

"Yeek!" Aaron says. "That's a bad word!"

"No," I say. "Sex is not a swear."

"What is 'sex'?" Alison asks.

"It means when people get naked and they kiss," Seth explains, laughing.

"When we talked about Snowflake mating with Smudge and having baby bunnies," I explain, "that's about sex. It's an important part of nature. And, Seth, you said, when we talked about Snowflake, that 'everybody comes from a mom.'"

"What if you say a swear in a way you would say thank-you?" Seth asks.

"If you were being friendly, you would probably use a more polite word," I tell him.

"Is it a swear if I hold up my middle finger when I mean the number one?" Alison asks.

"Absolutely not," I say. "You're not trying to be rude. But if you're trying to trick someone to get him in trouble, that would be rude." I look sternly at Seth.

"If you're holding a pencil and you take all your other fingers off before your middle finger," Kayla says, "that's not rude."

"One day, my dad was driving wicked fast," Daniel says, "and he cut in front of a lady and she put up her middle finger on purpose."

"She was being rude because she was angry at your dad," I say. "But we don't do that in school."

"When they prick your finger 'cause you're getting your blood tooken," Joel says, "it doesn't mean it."

"If all your fingers are hurt except your middle one," Aaron explains, "you can hold it up like that." He enjoys his demonstration.

"Well," Kathy says, "um. . . . I don't even know what the middle finger means."

"It's a symbol for making babies," I tell her.

"You can't put up the middle finger if you don't have one," Gregory points out.

"I think we've had enough examples," I tell him.

"What about crossing your fingers?" Joel asks.

"We'll talk about that another time," I say firmly. "It's time for math."

"If you use your middle finger—" Daniel begins.

I cut him off. "If you're interrupting math," I tell him, "it's definitely rude."

CHAPTER 30

The Car Race

"It's not fair!" Joel exclaims as he comes in from recess. "They're talking about Nina's car and not mine!" Spring has come, and the children are happy to be outdoors in their short sleeves, but I feel the tension as they come into the classroom.

"That's just because we like Nina's," Patrick explains bluntly, pointing to the car Nina made out of Legos.

"You don't like mine!" Joel exclaims. "We had a race and Nina's car won. I was being left out!"

"If people want to cheer for Nina, I think that's okay," Gregory answers. "Joel's car is still good. It doesn't mean his car is awful!"

Seth agrees. "I mean, I think it's okay to cheer for Nina, because Nina's car is cool."

I want to interrupt, to defend Joel, but I decide to give the discussion more time.

Nina speaks up. "Well, I was just doing a race. I didn't want to get into a big fight. And when people started saying that, I felt bad for Joel. But I didn't want to say anything, 'cause then they would just get into a bigger turbulation."

"I think it's okay to say something about Nina's car," Kathy says, " 'cause they didn't say, 'Oh, Nina's is the best and Joel's is dumbest.' I also think that if somebody's car wins, it doesn't mean they're the best; it just means they won. It doesn't mean like you're the worstest in the whole entire world if you don't win."

"If Nina's car wins the first time, it doesn't mean Joel's is always gonna lose, 'cause Joel's car could win sometimes," Gregory adds.

Alison takes a different view. "I think Joel is being left out, because everyone's talking about Nina's car. And Joel's car ran into a paper bag and Nina's didn't, and the paper bag stopped Joel's car. And I thought his car was pretty cool and I think he was left out."

Aaron agrees with her. "I think Joel's car sort of won," he says. "In baseball, if you get hit by the ball, you go to first base."

I'm glad I didn't intervene, after all. I would not have known about the paper bag.

To my surprise, Daniel supports Alison's idea.

"Maybe we should start the race over," he says, " 'cause Joel's car got stopped."

"I think now Nina's feeling kind of left out," Joel says, " 'cause Alison said my car is pretty cool."

"No," Nina answers. "I think it's fair, because before, everybody thought my car was the best. Now, everybody thinks Joel's car is."

"Let's start over," Seth agrees, " 'cause maybe it will be a tie!"

Travis adds, "We could have two groups. One will cheer for Nina and the other for Joel."

They quickly arrange the cheering sections for next recess, and we settle down for math.

CHAPTER 31

A Cold Duckling, a School Shooting, and a Home for a Dead Butterfly

The week Travis brought our four baby ducklings home for spring vacation, one of the ducklings died. The same week, two high school students went on a killing rampage in Littleton, Colorado.

At our morning meeting, first thing on Monday, the children are all talking at once, wanting to know what happened to the duckling. I quiet them down, and Travis speaks first.

"We took the duckling to my brother's school," he explains. "The good thing was, they gave me flowers. My brother's friend was holding one of the ducklings and it died because it couldn't breathe and we dug a grave and we gave it flowers and I visit it every day and say a prayer and that's all."

"When the duckling couldn't breathe, was it the flowers that made it?" Alison asks, trying to sort out the cause of death.

"No, the flowers were after the duckling died," Travis explains.

"Tuesday, last week, two people went into a high school with guns and weapons and shot twelve kids," Seth announces.

"And they shot one teacher," Gregory adds.

"Yeah," Seth agrees. "And then they shot theirselves."

" 'Cause they were so sad with what they did," Joel adds.

"How did you learn about it?" I ask.

"I went there," Seth answers. "I went to Colorado, where it happened."

The children look at him, surprised. "No," I tell him. "You

didn't." Later I thought of many better answers, but this is what I said.

"Well, I heard it on the news," he amends his story. "I came into the living room and Mom said, 'Come here,' and she told me about it and I thought she was lying till I heard it on the TV."

"I was watching a channel called TLC," Anna says, "and they have this show called *Medical Detective,* and there's this girl and her mom let her ride her bike down to the mailbox and a guy saw her and he knocked over her bike with his car and he just sort of stole her and killed her and scrambled her bones all around the desert."

"It's kind of funny," Kathy says, "because my mom saw a wedding and she thought it was a funeral."

"This girl," Alison says, "her mom was going somewhere to a house and she was going on a shortcut and she got runned over by a car and when they got home they didn't see her and the brother went off to find her and they drived off and they found her laying down and she was dead with her eyes open."

I am horrified to hear what they've been watching and I feel compelled to say something reassuring, although I don't know what would help them keep these bizarre images from overwhelming them. "When you see something on TV," I tell her, "and it feels too scary or it worries you, you can always ask Mom or Dad to change the channel."

"But we like it when it's scary!" Gregory says.

"I love it!" Seth says.

"I just *like* it." Gregory explains.

"I like it because it's exciting," Travis adds.

"I like it," Anna explains, "because I watch this channel, TLC, and it has lots of stuff like that, so I'm used to it by now and that's why I watch it on the news, too. I'm not afraid of blood anymore," she adds.

"I don't have many fears," Nina says, "and I know it wouldn't happen here, so I don't think I have to worry."

Clearly, these young children have been thinking about death more than I had realized.

————

A week later, I come into the room in the morning and find two of our four butterflies motionless on the bottom of the cage. I quickly sweep all four of them into a net and put them in the garden, watching two of the four fly away and land on the nearby bushes. I tell the children I let them go because I thought it was time for them to be free. I'd had enough of talk about death and imagined the kids had, too.

But a few days later, a group of children putting mulch on the garden find a butterfly on the ground, among our flowers. They show it to me, excitedly.

"It fluttered its wings!" Joel says. "I might have seen it flutter! No," he adds, looking carefully, "it was the wind."

"I think it's dead," Kayla says, peering at it. "It stayed that way for a long time."

"It's dead," Alison agrees. "Some of the yellow stuff is off its wings."

"Maybe it's just in a coma," Kayla says. "That means it goes to sleep but it's not dead."

Alison disagrees. "It would go somewhere safe if it was gonna go into a coma."

"No," Anna tells her firmly. "If it was gonna do a coma, it would do it right away."

"How can we tell if it's dead?" I ask.

"Is its heart beating?" Gregory asks. He puts his ear close to it.

"If it was dead," Alison says, "it would be kind of cold and it wouldn't just fly away. Its heart isn't beating and it has one wing out and one wing curled up."

"Well, yesterday, my dog killed a crow," Travis says, "and we went out to my yard to bury it and it was dead and it was still breathing and I thought it was dead so I touched it and I didn't know if its heart was beating. It's still lying in the same spot. It's kind of hot because it was a hot day out."

"I heard about a father and son," Joel says, "and they were buried and they were still alive and then they got buried 'cause the other people thought that they were dead. And then the father woke up and he couldn't breathe and he died."

The children are breathless with excitement, with this news.

"When the crow was dead," Travis says, "he lifted up one wing."

"I saw a dead chicken," Joel says, "and at the beginning when it's just dead it's not very stiff, but after it's been dead a while, it gets stiff."

"I'm going to pick the butterfly up," I say, "because I'm sure it's dead now. Do you want to hold it?"

Kayla takes it first. "We don't know where the heart is," she says, looking carefully. "It's warm and it's not stiff."

"It feels weird." Alison says, taking it from Kayla. "It's light. It's a little stiff but it's not moving. It doesn't flap its wings. I think it's dead."

"Can I make a little home for it?" Kathy asks. "A home outside with leaves and wood from nature?"

"Can I help? Can I help, too?" several children ask.

Seven children spend the next hour contentedly gathering leaves and flowers to build a home for the dead butterfly. I remember my attempt to avoid its death.

Maybe there's no way young children can make sense of the violent images of a school shooting, but perhaps I can start by helping them look at, touch, and talk about a dead butterfly.

Placing Blame

Jason's teacher shows me a letter Jason has written to the local paper:

Dear *Student Newsline* Editors:

I am very sad to hear about what happened in Littleton, Colorado. I was wondering ever since I heard about it what could make someone do something this awful. I have had several arguments in my head, which are these: The first argument is that it is the media's fault. But then I think of all the people who watch or listen to that stuff who don't go on massive killing sprees.

Another thing I was thinking about was whether it was the parents' fault or not. I think that it wasn't because when you are seventeen or eighteen your parents don't clean your room with you or go looking in your drawers. I think it would be fairly easy for the average 18-year-old to sneak a couple of machine guns into their house. But my dad said that if I only wore black, had no friends, and locked myself into my room every day for several hours playing Half-Life [a very violent computer game] he would start to worry.

Next, I was thinking about opinions and beliefs. I was online a while ago reading an article about a computer game named Carmageddon2: Carpocalypse Now. In Carmageddon2 you get points for running over innocent pedestrians and zoo animals.

People had written many letters in, saying three different types of things. The first type of letters were the type that say anyone who doesn't like Carmageddon is dumb because: number one, they haven't played it to see how fun it is, and number two, because you're not killing real people, just polygonal images. The second type said this: Carmageddon is a bad game because you're killing innocent people, but games where you kill "bad guys" are okay. The third kind of letter said that all kinds of killing in video games are bad, and they should all be banned.

I bet you are all wondering what my opinion is. So I'll tell you. It's kind of hard to say but I guess I think violent games are bad. While I am playing them I have fun. As a kid, I spend my time reading about them and playing them, my money is spent subscribing to magazines about them, my mind is absorbed into a web of violence, sex and profanity. No video game could make *me* bring a gun to school, but they may be different for other people. I don't think that parents should let their kids play these games, but if my parents said I couldn't have them I would be mad.

As hard as it is for me to believe that the author is only ten, I know that these are Jason's words.

Does he really believe he should not be allowed to play these violent games? Does he think they're bad for him, or just for others? Will he stop playing them?

And will his parents decide they need to set limits for him? With this last thought, I realize how concerned I feel about their approach. Do I hold them responsible for allowing him to become obsessed with this violent play, just as I blame the television viewing of my young ones on their parents' inability to turn off the TV? I remember nine-year-old Ross telling me, "What the parents should do is just say no, no, no, no, no, so they'll just give up. That's what they do to me, and I'm not violent."

I invite Jason to my room to talk, offer him some gummy worms, and put a box of Legos on the table. Jason likes to keep both his mouth and his hands busy while he thinks. I ask him how the Littleton shootings changed his opinion about violent computer games.

"Before it happened," he begins, chewing a worm and fiddling with the Legos, "I was sort of thinking about violence and computer games and I was thinking it didn't encourage violence. It just helped people blow off steam. I sort of don't think that anymore. I don't think that if you play a video game enough you'll want to kill someone, but I think it encourages it. Like I mean, when you're a kid, a lot of people yell at you and you get in trouble a lot and there's like people who are more important than you and people make fun of you. I mean a lot of stuff happens that probably made these kids feel uncomfortable and not so happy. Like you get bad grades in school or get in trouble or whatever, and if you get mad enough some people will take it the wrong way. Violent videos help people take it the wrong way, encourage them to be violent."

"What about somebody like you?" I ask.

"It's sort of weird," he answers. "Because I think they're bad, and I don't think they should be played by kids my age, but if I couldn't play them I'd be pretty mad, you know, so it's sort of weird. I like them and enjoy them but I don't think I should like them and enjoy them. I don't agree with myself on it, you know?

"I used to think they helped you take out violence. I don't think they really encourage violence for me. I don't have really enough aggression to make it necessary for me to have them, so like, they don't really do a good thing for me. But I don't think they do anything bad for me, either."

Is Jason simply justifying his own game-playing habits? If he does think they're bad for him, he may have to get rid of some games he likes or be agreeable to limits set by his parents. To say it's bad for other kids but not for him does not convince me, though I understand his dilemma. It's hard voluntarily to stay away from something so attractive.

"If you had more aggression," I ask him, puzzled by his last statement, "would violent games help you or make it worse?"

"It depends on how much," he answers. "Let's say I got yelled at a lot somewhere and I might get sort of mad and cause some aggression. Everywhere I went, people didn't like me and made fun of me and teased me. And people thought I was something bad. Then I think video games would be bad."

"So you're just on the okay side?" I ask. "You have enough bad feelings to make the games useful, but not so much they're dangerous?"

"I think so," he answers, chewing on a gummy worm. "Other

people might disagree with that. If I get home from school and I'm really mad at one of my teachers, I would play on the computer and feel a little bit better. But I don't know if that's true for everyone."

"Does it ever make you feel worse?" I ask.

"Sometimes if I don't do something right on a game and I screw up, I get mad at it. I'll probably stop for a while and try again later. Unless I did something very drastic that made me start the game all over. But maybe as I get older, that might not be true. It might have bad effects on me. When I get older, I might be really depressed or people might make fun of me, I don't know."

As Jason talks, his dilemma becomes clearer to me, and more poignant. For a kid who often feels powerless in relation to adults and to other kids, the video games are a safe way he can feel strong and in control. After a bad day at school, he can go to his room and peacefully kill off the enemies, making steady progress toward an attainable goal. With a video game, anyone can be a dominant puppy. It's a satisfaction in his life that he can count on. Why should he give it up? Yet he is afraid of his own anger and depression, and he knows that in another year he will face big changes. He'll have to leave the protection of his small school where he feels relatively safe and go to a middle school that is an unknown. If things got really bad, he wonders, could he lose control?

"Would you consider giving up your video games yourself?" I ask him.

"N . . . no," he answers slowly.

"What if your parents said you had to stop playing them?"

"I'd be pretty mad, probably for several months."

"Would it have been better if you had never started on them?"

"Maybe," he answers. "I don't know. I think that's sort of the wrong way to go, to completely shelter kids from it. Because when I meet little kids who are totally sheltered from violence, that just makes them have an incentive to do it. You want to do it 'cause you're not supposed to. I think that if a kid had a little bit of exposure to it and it wasn't encouraged or anything, I think it would be better than like letting him think he couldn't go near it.

"Games that have killing but the main purpose of the game isn't killing, it's action or puzzles or character interaction or something, that's what kind of game my parents let me play. If it's a game where you only see your gun and you go around shooting everyone and it's really gory and then the person laughs every time someone gets killed and there's screaming and stuff, no. But if it was a game where there's just a little person that blobs and goes 'pop,' that's not bad. What my dad says, and I agree with it, is that it's okay to have some violence as long as you keep talking about it and making sure that your kid knows that it's not a good thing. If you just leave it alone, he won't know any better."

When Jason first started telling me about this attitude, I thought it was an easy justification of his game playing. Now I am beginning to see his point. If his parents forbade his games, would he become more obsessed with his obsession?

I am impressed with how frequently Jason tells me his father's opinion. These conversations and the relationship that surrounds them are deeply meaningful to him. Could it be true that limiting the excessive violence and continuing this dialogue is a better middle ground than trying to eliminate the games altogether? Is this the equivalent, at age ten, of my effort to study violent play with my class, helping the children to make their own rules and to see the effects?

I am reminded of my effort to prohibit Barbie from entering my house when my daughter Sarah was four. I had made a dollhouse for her birthday, working in the basement at night after she was asleep. But as her birthday came closer, it became clear she was hoping for a Barbie doll. The night before her birthday, I explained that I thought Barbie looked like she did not get enough to eat, and that she looked like her feet must hurt in those high-heeled shoes. I said that I had other gifts for her birthday, and that I hoped she wouldn't be so disappointed she couldn't enjoy them.

"That's okay," she said cheerfully. "Veronica's giving me a Barbie at my party."

So Barbie entered our house, and with her came some of the best play I had seen. Barbie went to balls, changed clothes frequently, and played with many friends when visitors came over. When we went out to eat, Barbie, with a bag of dresses and tiny shoes, provided such good company that the adults could have a leisurely conversation and meal. At sixteen, Sarah still loves clothes and shoes, especially flowing medieval dresses, but has no wish to look like Barbie.

As the older children told me, clear limits are important. It is dangerous for the younger children who are not able to distinguish fantasy from reality to watch violence on television. I am convinced they need to deal with dead ducklings and butterflies before they can understand the images of a school shooting. But maybe I need to give up some of my rigidities in order to help children learn to make their own rules and understand the complexity of the world they will have to live in. Even if Jason gives up the most violent of his games, his fascination with them will remain. Perhaps his shelter lies not in hiding behind a big wing chair, but in the security of his continuing dialogue and relationship with his parents.

CHAPTER 33

Empathy

Ten years ago, still living in Chicago but teaching kindergarten with "normal" children, I went to an intensive weekend conference on group dynamics. I wanted to understand why, when I dislike groups so much, my working life centers on them. Should I, perhaps, get out of teaching and go into social work, where I could see my clients one at a time?

I didn't seem to be finding my answer during the weekend. On the last day, a rumor spread that a fat, unpleasant woman had left her own group as a result of a disagreement with the other members. We heard she was going from room to room, trying to find a group that would let her in. Our discussion was intense: if she came to us, should we allow her to join? People talked about boundaries, setting limits, and group cohesiveness. To my ear, calling her "the fat lady" and keeping her from our group was a form of prejudice and exclusion. I argued as persuasively as I could that if she came to us, we should take her in, but I could see the majority was against me. After the vote, I walked out, knowing that I could not be a part of a group that would call her names and get rid of her as my relatives had been labeled and herded away in Germany. As soon as I entered the hall and closed the door behind me, I realized I was now the fat lady. Having argued with my group and left it, I had no place to go. I would not knock on doors, begging to be let in. What would I do? I could go home early. My family, at least, would be glad to see me. But if I left without the last whole group session to help me clarify my experience, my weekend would have been wasted. I headed to the room with the coffeepot, needing the comfort of a warm drink and a place to sit and think. This was exactly what I hate most about being in a group: feeling out of control, with no way to change what seems to me to be a destructive path.

A young woman I recognized as coming from the same group walked in. She had decided to leave, too, and was uncertain of what to do next. Soon, an older woman joined us. Three! We could start a group of our own! The fat woman, if she existed, could make four.

We began to talk of our experiences at the conference, and what had brought us there. The young woman explained, "I am a counselor with emotionally disturbed children at the Orthogenic School." The older woman, looking as surprised as I felt, said, "I was a teacher there twenty years ago!" They were even more surprised when they realized that I had worked there at a time between the two of them.

What was it about our common experience that compelled us to risk spoiling our weekend by refusing to exclude an unwanted, unappealing person we had never met? Perhaps it was Bettelheim's conviction that no matter how strange or difficult another person's behavior, by looking honestly at our own feelings, we could find a common bond that would help us understand.

We talked and drank coffee until the small groups were over and we could go to the last meeting. I went to it elated. I could stand up against a destructive group and make a plan I would feel was right, whether or not others joined me.

It is true that I dislike groups when they use their power for exclusion and violence. I can't stand to watch the smiles of the observers as the heretics burn, or to hear the gleeful laugher of the suicide game. But there's nothing more exciting than riding that wave of energy and helping it focus on empathy and inclusion.

CHAPTER 34

A Big, Big Teacher

"What have you learned about your boys' love of violence?" the principal asks me on the last day of school as I pour my morning coffee. "Is there anything that I can pass on to their next teacher?"

I pause, realizing with surprise that I am not eager to pass these children on. Like a mother sending her child to school for the first time, I am afraid no one else will love and understand them as I do now.

"I still wish I could turn back the clock," I answer, "and insist the children be protected from violence until they are old enough to know the difference between fantasy and reality, even when they are immersed in their play. We flood our children with violent images, and then we do not want them to express their reactions through play, as children will do when they need to deal with experiences that are important to them. Imagine what would happen if you told the teachers that talking or even thinking about the Littleton shootings would turn us into aggressive and potentially dangerous adults! At the same time, the children need to learn to articulate their feelings about their play, to listen to each other and to make rules that will help them treat each other with empathy and respect.

"There's a six-year-old who might be in your class next year," she tells me, "who stays up until ten-thirty at night to watch *South Park*."

"What's that?" I ask.

"It's a program where a boy gets killed in a different violent way at the end of each episode. It's a spoof with sex, violence, and prejudice," she explains.

Maybe he could go to the other class, I tell myself. Don't I deserve a break?

An hour later, the children are telling me their last stories of the year. I look at the list of children who have signed up for this activity, and see TRAVIS, his large and shaky but legible printing near the top of the list.

I am so proud of Travis, the youngest child in the class. In September, he could not remember any of the letters in his name. He did not know what he wanted to play and he let his friends take his turn for him when he played a board game. Now he loves to tell stories and he writes his own name on the list.

Travis stands next to me at the table, ready to tell his story. "Travis is the teacher," he begins. "One time, I was a big, big teacher. And then three people came into the classroom, so I started making a poster."

In his pause, I take delight in his beginning. Travis used to say, "I can't remember," to most questions. Now he can imagine himself as a big teacher. I decide to make a collection of the children's last stories, and give a copy to each child in the class as a memento of our difficult but satisfying year together.

I expect the poster Travis, as teacher, is making with his students is about the alphabet. He is so proud of the letters he has learned. "What's on the poster?" I ask him, eager to check my theory.

"Guns and weapons," he answers.

I don't have to write that down, I decide quickly. It's part of our conversation, not part of his story.

I look up at Travis, standing beside me. He looks confident, wearing a small suit of camouflage, with a plastic walkie-talkie hanging from his belt and army green binoculars slung around his neck. His smile, beaming at me, exudes goodwill.

"What happens next?" I ask, hoping he will forget about the guns and weapons and return to his original plot.

"The teacher got killed," he answers. "And then they all got shot."

My heart sinks as I write down his words. I will not collect the stories to give to the children. I will just give a copy to the principal.

Looking at Travis, I remember the photograph of myself, wearing my leather cowgirl vest and hat, holding a cap gun in each hand and ready to shoot the Lone Ranger's enemies on the television screen. I wanted to be powerful and strong. I would never have imagined being dead.

I wonder if Travis will act this story out with the hushed tragedy of our Littleton discussions or with the slapstick humor of the suicide game. I feel my curiosity begin to build, as my disappointment is replaced by a new set of questions. Why would Travis want to be a dead teacher? I wonder if turning death into slapstick comedy makes it less frightening, or whether children who are too young to understand the permanence of death find it easy to laugh about it.

Maybe next year, the boy who watches *South Park* will help me understand.

The school year over, I travel to my parents' home where my family still loves to spend the summer. In the attic, I notice the desk that holds jumbled piles of old family photographs. I start to rummage through the drawers, pausing at the picture of my father, young and handsome in his wartime uniform, and of me in my first grade school photo, with several front teeth missing. I begin to search for the picture I remember, the one where I hid behind the chair, afraid to watch the television. My first glimpse of the old black-and-white print delights me. Just as I had remembered, I am wearing my cowgirl hat, my eyes are riveted on the television that is just out of view. But to my surprise, I am not hiding behind the chair. Instead, I am sitting up straight, my hand is ready to pull my cap gun out of my holster, and I ride the hassock like a palomino.

Epilogue

I sit at the breakfast table one year after the Littleton tragedy when a headline in the *New York Times* catches my eye: "Parents Find Rules for Play Have Changed in New Jersey." I read on. Four kindergartners have been suspended for pretending to shoot one another with their fingers.

"Dr. B.," I muse as I shake my head. "What would you say to this?"

"So," answers a familiar German accent in my ear. "You are surprised? It vas so easy for you, whom I taught myself, to look at your feelings about violence, that you expect these teachers and administrators can so quickly face their own?" He sits down across the table from me, raises one eyebrow, and gives me a half smile, indicating that I, too, am no more ignorant than he would have expected.

"You're right, of course," I tell him. He nods with an irritatingly smug smile. "At staff meeting last week," I continue, "with all the parental concern about violence, several teachers wanted to prohibit children from bringing any toys to school except stuffed animals and dolls. They were offended by Travis's camouflage pants, army green binoculars, and walkie-talkie at recess and they believed that such toys distracted the children from learning in the classroom. I argued that this would be unfair. A girl could spank her doll to her heart's content—why couldn't Travis communicate through a walkie-talkie? Then the teachers considered banning all toys from home. This ban, at least, would apply the new rule equally to both boys and girls. It wasn't until I got home that I realized I had not given one of my most important arguments: that through our discussions about their toys, the children develop their ability to express their feelings and to realize that other people have interesting ideas that are different from their own."

"If this is so important, vhy did you forget it?" Dr. B. looks serious now, his eyebrows knit together in a frown, watching as I search my soul.

"There's a part of me that agrees that it would be so much easier to have no toys from home," I confess. "It takes time and energy to deal with each incident, each cry of 'unfair' when a child doesn't share or when someone feels left out. The quick solution is so attractive: No pretend shooting! No Popsicle stick weapons! No talk of suicide! I have to remind myself that each time I insisted that the children solve a problem concerning exclusion or violent play they came up with a solution, one that respected both sides of the issue. I think of Joel's half bulldog, half Chihuahua that gave him a valued role in the game of house, Nina's recess rule that prohibited violent fantasies at alternate recesses, and Seth's twenty-bolt fence that protected him from disappointment. But by the time I remembered the quick rule was accepted and the opportunity past."

"Each time you rethink these lessons, it vill help you prepare for the future," Dr. B. answers. "Next time, you may remember your argument sooner—perhaps in the car on the vay home. Eventually, you vill have these thoughts during the discussion or you may even be able to anticipate the problem and be ready for it. The vish to avoid our most difficult feelings is always present," he adds more gently. "Vhat is important is to continue to be avare of that denial."

"One thing I have learned," I tell him, "is the importance of making a clear distinction between pretend violence and behavior that truly hurts or frightens children. Pretend violence, like pointing a finger and saying 'bang' while a friend falls on the ground, does not hurt anyone, and the rules can be negotiated by everyone involved in the game. Real violence hurts bodies or feelings, is frightening, and is often closely connected with exclusion.

"But this leads to an issue I find harder to think clearly about: the connection between violence and exclusion. When I first started audiotaping the children's play and talk, I cut out every discussion about exclusion. I thought it did not relate to my subject of violence. But when exclusion kept coming up, I decided to listen to those discussions, and I found that exclusion and violence seemed to be inextricably intertwined. Excluding someone from the group seemed to justify violence, both by the excluded child and by those who exclude him, just as when Seth and Patrick called Joel a baby before knocking him down and when Caleb called Nate a girl before punching him. On the other hand, as Jason described and as we learned from the killers at Columbine, the excluded child can feel justified in using violence to hurt those who exclude him. I wish I could just tell the children to be more inclusive, but it's never that easy.

"Each time a new issue comes up," I continue, "I have to remind myself that empathy must include a willingness to look at anger as well as affection. I feel as though I should know that by now."

"If it vas so easy, the vorld vould not be in the mess it's in now," Dr. B. answers, waving a hand toward my newspaper. I glance at the headline, and by the time I look up, he has disappeared: those silent, rubber-soled shoes again. I breathe deeply, reassured that although I have far to go, I have not failed. I could bring up the no-toys rule at our next faculty meeting. Or perhaps, like Jason, I'll keep my eyes open, waiting to see what will frighten me next.

ACKNOWLEDGMENTS

Above all, I am grateful to Jed, Margaret, and Hannah for their un-limited support and their cheerful willingness to do whatever was needed to help me with the writing of this book.

I would like to thank Eli Schmitt and Colby Eck for helping me understand what it is like to be a boy in today's world.

I am indebted to Jorie Hunken for being there to listen when I felt stuck, and to the Still River Writers for teaching and support-ing me.

Finally, I would like to express my appreciation to Dick Zaj-chowski and Touchstone Community School for encouraging me in this project.